THE PROVING GROUNDS

MICHAEL BOYD

DIZZY EMU PUBLISHING

1714 N McCadden Place, Hollywood, Los Angeles 90028

www.dizzyemupublishing.com

THE PROVING GROUNDS

MICHAEL BOYD

ISBN-13: 978-1540418319

First published in the United States

in 2016 by Dizzy Emu Publishing

www.dizzyemupublishing.com

THE PROVING GROUNDS

BY

MICHAEL BOYD

(A SCREENPLAY)

(CONTINUED)

CONTINUED:

Open on: black. Small red titles appear on the black background. We hear soft blowing wind and dust over this.

1 EXT. NEVADA DESERT. DAY. 1

Fade in: Slowly to a massive panorama of the Nevada desert. Shrubs and tumble weeds stir and tumble in a light breeze. We hold on this for a while. Next the ground five miles away from the camera erupts. The perfect circle shock wave starts to decimate the surroundings. The mushroom cloud takes full form and melts clouds in the sky. The shock wave draws closer to:

Camera tracks back to reveal: Twenty soldiers all sit in lines in a huddle on the ground with sun glasses. Camera tracks back until a pair of glasses are flung away and hands cover their owners eyes making the shot black, whose POV we are now seeing. Soon this is illuminated in fiery red and orange as the intensity of the light shines through and shows the soldiers' flesh, allowing him and us to see the veins and bones in his hand.

Here the titles appear.

The Proving Grounds

The shot and titles fade with the bomb's dying light.

FADE TO BLACK:

2 EXT. NEVADA DESERT. DAY. 2

Camera is met with blazing sunlight and the impression of blistering heat, desert flora and fauna and sonic desert ambience.

Although this flora and fauna is not as it should be. An eyeless and shocking pink snake slithers by, his pre-mature skin sliding off as he goes revealing raw moist undeveloped skin underneath his prematurely shed layer.

Next is a cactus, where the body is one big thorn.

Camera focusses on one of the strange flowers, moves away along the desert floor for a beat or two and then tilts up to reveal the next scene.

3 EXT. SMALL DESERT RESIDENCES. DAY. 3

Camera on the same level as the sun stares into the gleaming globe surrounded by cloudless blue sky.

Two grizzled desert men carrying dead prairie dogs look at their former home in the crushed pile of old caravans, they also see impressions in the ground where the caravans were. The area is also littered with trash. The two men are: **HARRY** and his **FATHER**. **HARRY** (30s) Hispanic cold looking man in old clothes. His **FATHER** (70s) in even more decrepit clothes and has a white beard.

A nuclear war head hangs down from the top of a tall thin scaffolding structure. A purpose built nuclear village can be seen in the distance as well.

A yellow sign with the radioactive logo on it is propped up on a wooden stake a few yards away. The sign's text reads: Property of US Government. Weapons Testing. Keep Out.

HARRY looks at the sign, his face deadpan.

HARRY takes out some keys and throws them down.

DISSOLVE TO:

4 EXT. NEVADA DESERT. DAY. 4

We see the men trudging through the desert.

DISSOLVE TO:

5 EXT. NEVADA DESERT. NIGHT. 5

They have set up a camp.

The pair of them sit round their unlit fire. **FATHER** takes out a lighter and a tin of roll-up cigarettes, takes a cigarette with his mouth, lights it, takes a deep drag on it then exhales and the smoke disappears quickly in a desert zephyr then lights the fire with the lighter.

A bit later:

5 CONTINUED: 5

The two of them have their two prairie dogs on the fire, and are tearing off chunks of flesh and eating it.

6 EXT. NEVADA DESERT. EARLY MORNING. 6

HARRY and **FATHER** are asleep, next **HARRY** wakes with a start. He sits looking around for a beat. The fire has gone out. **HARRY** cracks his jaw and neck, then stretches.

HARRY walks over to a cactus and tears a hand off. He removes the thorns, bites into it and drinks its water deeply. He walks back and kicks his father.

FATHER
Don't fucking kick me boy!

HARRY
It's cooler at this time.

FATHER reluctantly gets up. When he has found his bearings he sees that **HARRY** has already started walking and is out in front. His **FATHER** doesn't hurry, he just shuffles slowly behind.

Close shot: A rattle snake in a coil, and **FATHER's** foot drawing closer.

HARRY turns round when he hears a yelp from his **FATHER. HARRY** walks up to his **FATHER.** When he gets there, his **FATHER** slugs him across the face.

FATHER
You Goddamn fucking lousy, useless cocksucking... cocksucker! You're meant to look out for fucking these fucking things!

His **FATHER** is grabbing and pushing him, **HARRY** pushes him to the ground in annoyance. **FATHER** clutches his leg screaming on the ground. **HARRY** sees two red holes in his Father's leg. He turns round and sees the hissing rattlesnake responsible. In a lightning flash **HARRY** stands on the snake, the snake bits his shoe and **HARRY** stamps on the snake's head killing it. He tears off the rattle. Two holes are now in **HARRY'S** shoe. **HARRY** shakes the rattle at his father as proof of its passing.

FATHER
Bind ma leg... I-I said bind the Goddamn thing.

6 CONTINUED: 6

HARRY doesn't, he looks around, his face sort of bewildered looking. **HARRY** turns. He looks down blank faced at **FATHER. FATHER** looks up at **HARRY.**

FATHER
Wh-what the fuck ya doin' boy? I said what't fuck are y'doin'?

HARRY continues to glance at his father. **HARRY** kneels down beside his **FATHER. HARRY** takes **FATHER'S** neck in his hands. **HARRY** is met by terror and struggling from **FATHER. HARRY** is too strong and three visceral cracks later, **FATHER'S** neck is broken. **HARRY** takes all his father's belongings.

Next **HARRY** pulls the corpse over to a rock, where he bends the arm unnaturally over a rock. **HARRY** takes a sharp rock and stands above his **FATHER'S** arm. He raises the rock above his head, he brings it down breaking the joint open. **HARRY** gets Sparked with blood.

HARRY proceeds to munch zealously on the arm. This is seen in a series of shots. He wipes his mouth with his sleeve. He munches on his viscera and stares out into the endless desert.

7 EXT. NEVADA DESERT. NIGHT. 7

HARRY wanders the vast extents of the desert, just walking, up close and in the distance this strange figure keeps moving carrying the arm on his relentless unknown journey.

HARRY sits and rests. He shields his eyes from an extremely bright flash.

A terrible distant roaring and rumbling makes **HARRY** recoil. A rolling dust storm heads towards him, he flinches and ducks as it hits him, a great and terrible wind blows dust across the plain. **HARRY** falls to his feet and protects his face. This dust storm does not last long, and the valley soon calms down again.

DISSOLVE TO:

8 EXT. NEVADA DESERT. DAY. 8

HARRY is seen walking through a heat shimmer. He has a small beard now.

Close on **HARRY:** He is drenched with sweat.

HARRY trips up and looks at what he tripped over. It is the disturbed edge of a desert dirt track. It goes on as far as **HARRY** can see in both directions. He looks down one, and then the other. **HARRY** chooses a direction and heads down it.

JUMP CUT TO:

Much further down the track and not one car passes.

Close on: spinning station wagon tyre and hub cap barreling down the desert track reflecting what it passes. Luggage on roof an inside, a family with a child barrel past **HARRY. HARRY** puts his thumb out to hitchhike, they don't stop, **HARRY** continues to look on in the car's direction, annoyed in his own way.

CUT TO:

9 EXT. NEVADA DESERT. DAY. 9

The car we saw pass **HARRY** lies trashed on the side of the road. The car doors are all open.

HARRY walks along the track and sees the car that passed him in the distance and looks mystified.

He arrives at the car; looks inside, there is blood everywhere, the interiors raided and trashed the male driver's head impaled on the steering wheel.

HARRY hears commotion off in the desert a bit. He stands up from his inspection.

There are two other cars about thirty yards in front of the station wagon with jump-wires connecting them, they are unmanned.

9 CONTINUED: 9

HARRY sees quite far off, a band of men running around, jeering and laughing. Beating and taunting a little girl, he walks towards them.

As **HARRY** draws even closer, the men look round, one holds the girl in a vice grip. **HARRY** looks blankly at them. Another of them walks up to **HARRY** and waves a pump-action shotgun in his face. **HARRY** remains completely calm.

THUG
What you lookin' at bitch?

THUG makes wimpish feminine sounds.

HARRY
You...

THUG
You bein' smart boy? You talkin' back to me?-

The **THUG** moves closer.

THUG
-You wanna die boy?

HARRY
...

THUG
Why don't you jist go back t'your business and keep walkin', and forget you poked your pecker into somethin' that aint yar business anyways?... Or is it, you wanna piece? Is that it bitch?

Other **THUGS** laugh.

THUG
Well you aint git'n any o' what isn't yours... I says boy you got yirself an ass on ya'. Jist like ma daddy says, holes hole, don't mitter whit age-

(Gestures to child).

THUG
-or which one, holes hole. Older min ain't too bad neither!

9 CONTINUED: (2) 9

The **THUG** takes one hand to unzip his fly. **HARRY** puts his hand into his pocket, which makes the gang point their guns at him. Regardless **HARRY** resumes taking his snake rattle out of his pocket. The **THUGS** laugh.

THUG 2
Whit ya gonna do wit' that? Rattle us t'sleep?

THUGS raucously laugh for a moment then go back to silence.

HARRY stares the **THUG** unrelentingly in the face. The **THUG** stares back. **HARRY'S** face remains the same in this sequence. **HARRY** rattles the rattle. The **THUG** for a split second looks down at the rattle, just what **HARRY** was wanting.

HARRY dashes forward into the **THUG.** He elbows the **THUG** in the stomach devastatingly hard that saliva is ejected forward. **HARRY** grabs the shot-gun in the **THUG'S** hand bashing the **THUG'S** head with the butt, and using the **THUG** as a human shield to the other attacker's bullets, the bullets fly into the back of **HARRY'S** human shield and kill the **THUG** he is using. **HARRY** is nicked by a bullet in the arm, he yelps in rage at this. **HARRY** rapidly blows the others away, except for one, aiming for their heads and torsoes.

REMAINING THUG
Turn round! I said turn round!. I wanna see your face when ya die.

HARRY lurches round, and slashes the **REMAINING THUG'S** throat with his finger nails leaving some slashes. Blood pours out of them. The **REMAINING THUG** reels back gurgling. He falls over. **HARRY** walks towards him.

JUMP CUT TO:

HARRY approaches the girl. **HARRY** picks her up with one arm and looks at her like she was an alien.

10 EXT. NEVADA DESERT. DAY. 10

HARRY walks over to the truck the keys belong to. He throws the girl in.

11 INT. THUG'S TRUCK. DAY. 11

HARRY'S hairy masculine arm is covered in blood.

He has bound his arm with shreds of his clothing.

12 EXT. TRUCK. NEVADA DESERT. DAY 12

HARRY grimaces as if he is in discomfort. He turns on the car heating onto full and sits and basks in the car's heat, despite it being a scorching 45 degrees Celsius.

Next **HARRY** takes out the rattle snake rattle and rattles it as if he were a fanatical baby.

13 EXT. NEVADA DESERT. DAY. 13

HARRY drives the pick up truck away with him and the girl in the front and one of the bodies of the thugs in the back of the truck. He drives it into the desert.

DISSOLVE TO:

14 EXT. NEVADA DESERT. NIGHT. 14

With their truck nearby, **HARRY** sits at the fire. The girl lies near by, sleeping. One of the thugs is cooking on the fire, his torso charred. **HARRY** eats a chunk of him.

HARRY
What's your name?

The girl is woken by this, she is confused and fearful and doesn't respond, she starts to crawl away. **HARRY** leans over and pulls her closer to him.

HARRY
(Irritated.)
What's your name?

BABY NANCY
Ancy.

HARRY
(Screws up his face.)
What?

14 CONTINUED: 14

BABY NANCY
N-N-N-Nancy.

HARRY nods vaguely to himself. He leans over and tears off a chunk of flesh off the corpse and hands it to her. She looks at him in a worried fashion. **HARRY** gestures at her to eat.

BABY NANCY still looks at him.

HARRY
(Quietly but emphatically.)
EAT! You need to eat! Stupid bitch.

BABY NANCY takes a coy nibble. And then eats more zealously.

Camera jumps back from them, and sees them munching away on the thug meat.

DISSOLVE TO:

15 EXT. NEVADA DESERT. DAY. BLISTERING HEAT. 15

A shot of some wheel-less cars are seen. They are rusting and peeling.

A shot of an old 1950's gas station is seen.

One of the strange snakes slithers along the ground next to a pump.

The establishment as a whole is seen. **HARRY'S** hand with the rattle comes into shot. The rattle is rattled.

CUT TO BLACK:

EXT. NEVADA DESERT. DAY.

The screen remains black for a few moments.

Fade in

15 CONTINUED: 15

A strange metallic sky is seen, bright blue sky with white clouds. Camera elevates up above, to reveal that the shot was a reflection of the sky in a car roof. The car accelerates along a desert road.

We can see it's the early 70's from the clothes and car. Five teenagers are stuffed into a small car. One of which is **WESTON LEWIS. WESTON** sits in the back seat squashed up against one of the back doors. He has a cool tight cheesecloth shirt, aviators and flares. He takes a large swig out of a bottle of water. **WESTON** twitches with Tourette's Syndrome.

WESTON has tuned out from what his friends are saying. He hears all the sounds of the car and the outside but he only sees the moving mouths of his friends. Like aural negative space. He takes a picture out of his pocket. It has a picture of an elderly woman on in. **WESTON** touches the picture and smiles gently. He takes out a pen and writes R.I.P. On the bottom of it.

The folks in the car have kind of drifted off. A siren is heard a way in front of their car. **WESTON** looks round smiling. His smile soon disappears when he looks out of the window and sees a diversion. The friends in the car grumble irritably.

KURT
Ugh, what the fuck are pigs doing here?

The car slows down in front of the police and the police diversion.

KURT rolls the car up to the police man.

KURT
(Rolls window down.)
What seems to be the problem officer?

A huge black man with all in one shades and chewing tobacco in his mouth walks up to the window.

OFFICER
Where you boys headin'

KURT
Vegas sir.

15 CONTINUED: (2) 15

The **OFFICER** clicks the tobacco in his mouth in acknowledgement.

OFFICER
Ah see, you can't come down this road, weapons testing is about to begin here, but that way down there is the diversion, and you'll get to Vegas that way.

WESTON pulls his window down and speaks to the officer.

WESTON
But officer, that way just leads into the desert.

OFFICER
Are you callin' me a liar? BOY!

WESTON is a little frightened by this.

WESTON
No sir, I just mean, there aren't any markings on the road, and we could easily get lost.

OFFICER
If you had let me finish and shut the fuck up you'd have heard me say, there's another checkpoint about five miles straight, you'll get to Vegas that way.

WESTON
Yes, sir. Sorry sir.

The **OFFICER** gestures with his head, and the car starts off.

The **OFFICER** picks up his walkie-talkie.

OFFICER
They're comin' now Harry.

Crackly and distorted reply over Walkie Talkie.

HARRY
About time.

(Voice disconnects).

15 CONTINUED: (3) 15

The **OFFICER** looks on at the car in the distance.

CUT TO:

16 INT. KURT'S CAR. DAY. 16

MICK
What the fuck was that all about?

WESTON
I just didn't think it was right sending us off down an unmarked trail. He had no cause to speak to us like that.

KURT has a draw on his asthma inhaler. **HENRY** lights up a cigarette. **WESTON** waves the smoke away with his hand.

HENRY
WHAT!?

WESTON shakes his head but does not say anything.

DISSOLVE TO:

17 EXT. NEVADA DESERT. DAY. 17

JUMP CUT:

The car drives through desert and desert and desert, but reaches no check-point. The car begins to travel more slowly as the terrain become more bumpy. Inside the car they are all arguing.

WESTON
I knew that policeman was talkin' out his ass.

HENRY
I told you we should have just gone back onto the road a few miles down.

KURT
Just shut the fuck up right! That would have been illegal.

MICK
But if they're phony doughnuts then it isn't.

(CONTINUED)

17 CONTINUED: 17

KURT
Just shut up!

WESTON
Can we turn back Kurt, follow our tracks back?

KURT
No, the wind would have killed them after two miles.

WESTON
Well what the hell are we going to do?

KURT
Listen I don't have all the fucking answers-

WESTON
Look?

ALTOGETHER
WHAT?

WESTON
Look, there's a truck behind us, maybe they can help, maybe he's come down the diversion too?

KURT
Yeah, I'll pull over.

WESTON
Yeah...No wait!

KURT
WHAT?

WESTON
He's coming at us very...VERY FUCKING FAST!!!

HENRY looks round.

HENRY
What the fuck?

WESTON looks round very panicked.

WESTON
Kurt keep going! Just keep on going... FASTER!

18 EXT. NEVADA DESERT. DAY. 18

A massive dirty wheel spins at about 130MPH, a great hulking 4x4 off road reinforced bull bar truck charges along the desert, crushing all the shrubbery in its path. The windows are so dirty, the driver is almost invisible. Billows of black and blue exhaust spew out of two tower exhaust pipes.

KURT tries to swerve and go off in a slightly different direction, but the massive truck just turns towards them again.

19 INT. KURT'S CAR. DAY. 19

Back with the friends, they have broken into frenetic tears and panic. They are all screaming at **KURT** to drive faster, but he can't due to the surface of the desert.

One of the front tires bursts. The screaming and panicking in the car elevates to an unbearable level.

20 EXT. NEVADA DESERT. DAY. 20

The vehicular aggressor collides brutally at an angle with Kurt's car, writing it off and bringing it to a grinding halt.

The massive truck slides to a clumsy stop. One of it's door opens and a small but deadly little man who is **GRABLE** runs out with a baton, (we move very quickly and don't see him clearly), he smashes a window of the car.

WESTON who is bleeding slightly is very shaken up. His face displays dismay and shock.

All the men wear dark blue mechanic overalls and we do not see their backs. The maniac we saw at the beginning, who is called **HARRY** (who is now around 20 years older and in his early 50's with graying hair and stubble) opens a door of the truck and steps out tearing meat off a chicken drumstick. He and his men walk up to the wreckage and go about knocking out the survivors. **WESTON** who is upside down and bleeding, moans when he sees the intimidating silhouette approach him. Baton hits screen.

20 CONTINUED: 20

HARRY

Let's go.

HARRY and two of his men **GRABLE** and **DOMINIC SUNSET** (who wears a gas mask) all walk back round into the truck and drive away. The wrecked car is in the foreground and blows up into flames after a few beats.

DISSOLVE TO:

21 INT. METAL CHAMBER. TIME OF DAY UNKNOWN. 21

The burning car dissolves into **HARRY'S** metal cigarette lighter. **HARRY** stands in a blackened metal room.

Camera sees all the friends from the car chained to metal chairs in this chamber. The two fake policemen from the fake diversion are there with **HARRY** and his men **CASTLE BRAVO** and **IVY MIKE. DOMINIC SUNSET**, someone from **HARRY'S** truck, wears a gas mask and walks up to all the hostages with a canister of petrol.

WESTON'S face displays mortal terror. His head is darting around looking everywhere.

WESTON

Please, we won't tell anyone!!! What did we do? I'm sorry, we're sorry!!! Please!!! I swear upon everything I love, I won't tell anyone, I don't want to tell anyone, I'm not interested in anyones' business or getting anyone in trouble or anything. I would never do that!!!

DOMINIC SUNSET opens the canister and pours the golden-pink fuel over all the people in the chairs. The friends cough and gag at the acrid petrol fumes.

WESTON breaks into tears and violent sobs shakes and spasms around. His tourette's is going crazy here. He is also trying to desperately avoid the petrol.

WESTON

Please, please, stop, please.

WESTON and his friends are sobbing violently and are begging for mercy as they are splashed with petrol.

After **DOMINIC SUNSET** finishes dousing them, he takes a broom and sweeps away the linking rivers of petrol on the ground.

HARRY flicks his lighter on and off over and over, some of the friends vomit with the fear. **HARRY** does not smile and does not physically look like he is enjoying it. But he is under his inscrutable exterior.

HARRY walks up to **MICK. WESTON** and his friends turn their heads and watch.

WESTON
D-d--don't hurt him, leave him alone!!!!

GRABLE walks up and punches **WESTON** across the jaw. **WESTON** spits out a mouthful of blood, and a tooth, he shakes in pain.

WESTON
(In a tourette's spasm.)
Fuck, fuck, shit, cunt, Chink, Nip, Gook, Wog, Nigger, Honkey!

GRABLE
Shut up!

WESTON'S friends lament and plead with their captors.

KURT
What do you want? Please let-

MICK
-We'll do anything you want, we won't tell a soul, please!!

WESTON
It's not in our interest to tell anyone, please just let us go.

GRABLE gives **WESTON** a back-hand slap. **WESTON** sobs into his lap, trying to conceal his tourette's. **GRABLE** looks at him scathingly. **MICK** is rocking back and forth in panic.

HARRY
What are you?

MICK
W-what?

21 CONTINUED: (2) 21

HARRY
What are you?

MICK
I-I don't-

HARRY puts his face at point blank range to **MICK.**

HARRY
WHAT ARE YOU!!!!

MICK
I DUNNO! I DUNNO, UH...UH... A MAN? A PERSON? A HUMAN?

HARRY
(Rolls his eyes.)
How do you make a living and what grades did you get in school?

MICK
I'm majoring in classics, I'm going to be a Lawyer.

HARRY rolls his eyes and gets his lighter out, at this sight the friends spasm in terror. **HARRY** moves the lighter to **MICK'S** chin, the fumes catch light a few inches a way, **MICK** goes up in flames as if he were dry leaves, and he stops rocking back and forth and starts to thrash violently and scream in pain. While this is happening **HARRY** moves onto the next person who is **HENRY. HENRY** shakes his head and pleads.

The chamber is really hot now, all the captives are drenched and glistening with sweat. **HARRY** and his men are not sweating at all.

Camera sees a trail of petrol run along the ground from **MICK** to **HENRY.** The trail ignites **HENRY.** He also begins to wail and lament and thrash in agonising pain. He emits choked, guttural and truly inhuman voice tearing, sickening bellows.

KURT
(Hopelessly.)
I don't know what you want, please I don't know, I don't know.

HARRY
What are you?

21 CONTINUED: (3) 21

KURT
(Sobbing.)
I don't know.

HARRY
Do you know anything about science?

WESTON looks round in shock. **WESTON** looks nervously at **KURT** who is too terrified to really make any sense of anything. He just continues to shake his head and beg for mercy.

WESTON
I-I do, I do!

There is so much noise with the two burning screaming friends, that **HARRY** does not hear **WESTON.** But **GRABLE** does.

GRABLE
Shut the fuck up!!!!

GRABLE hits **WESTON** again.

WESTON continues.

WESTON
(In choaked vehement bellows)
I DO! I KNOW!- I KNOWWW!!!
WAIIIIIITTTT!!!!

GRABLE punches **WESTON** in the stomach winding **WESTON. WESTON** tries further to shout, but can only mouth, he panics and has great difficulty breathing. The two remaining friends **WESTON** and **KURT** have difficulty breathing with the heat and fumes. Sparks erupt with the petrol fumes igniting in the air.

KURT cannot control himself with the terror and throws up in front of **HARRY, HARRY** gets some on his work-boot. **HARRY** looks at it with thought and then looks away. **HARRY** takes his lighter out again and sets **KURT** on fire too.

KURT joins the now quickly dying cacophony of burning death and screaming. **HARRY** signals to one of his men to extinguish **KURT, GRABLE** does so with a fire extinguisher. **KURT** is devastatingly injured with 3rd degree burns.

(CONTINUED)

21 CONTINUED: (4) 21

But he is out cold and **WESTON** can see him still breathing slightly.

HARRY looks back at and walks towards **WESTON. WESTON** looks petrified and quivers a little, his tourette's gets even worse here. **HARRY** kneels down in front of **WESTON. WESTON** blinks rapidly and makes some eye-twitches. **HARRY** just looks at him for a short while.

HARRY
What do you know about detonators.

WESTON
S-s-some s-stuff.

HARRY
How do you fix it if it's broken?

WESTON
It's like r-r-re setting a-a clock
if it's faulty, it's quite a-a-a s-
simple m-m-mechanism.

HARRY
How do you know.

WESTON
We uh- studied mining technology
at my university, explosives were
a part of that.

HARRY stands back. He thinks about something whilst looking at **WESTON.**

KURT
(Strained, croacky
and pained.)
LEAVE US ALOONNNEEEEE!!!!!!!

GRABLE boots **KURT** in the chest so hard, that he coughs up blood. **GRABLE** reaches into **KURT'S** mouth and tears out his tongue and throws it down sizzling on the burning metal floor. **KURT** passes out in shock again blood cascading from his swollen and traumatised mouth.

HARRY lights his lighter.

WESTON
(In crippling
strained sobs.)
OH GOD!!!... HELP US!!... PLEASE
SOMEBODY... SAVE US!!!!

21 CONTINUED: (5) 21

HARRY looks like he is going to ignite **WESTON**, but stops just before he does.

HARRY gestures at **CASTLE BRAVO**, to untie **KURT**, which he does.

HARRY
Castle Bravo,...

HARRY nods his head at **CASTLE BRAVO.**

CASTLE BRAVO hauls **KURT** away out of the chamber. Leaving only **HARRY** and **WESTON, HARRY** slowly turns to face **WESTON.** We see **WESTON'S** reaction to this.

22 EXT. THE REAR OF HARRY'S GARAGE. EVENING. 22

HARRY marches **WESTON** round the back of the metal chamber which is near **HARRY'S** garage, where a huge vintage motorbike sits. **HARRY** stuffs the key's in **WESTON's** hands.

HARRY gives **WESTON** a look which says exactly what will happen if he does not do whatever it is he has been told to do. **WESTON** desperately acknowledges this and shuffles over to a motor bike

WESTON cries while the bike speeds along the track back into the desert.

FADE IN:

23 EXT. NEVADA DESERT. DUSK. 23

A far away camera sees a little car speeding along the windy desert track we just saw **WESTON** speeding along.

Shot of the car front on speeding along the road is seen.

Inside the cab we meet, **LUTHER TELLER.** A strangely attractive, slim man (20s) who looks very tired and washed out and is bald. He wears a gradient shirt, starting at fiery orange and ascending into violet towards the neck.

(CONTINUED)

23 CONTINUED: 23

LUTHER has a little thermometer hanging from his mirror. It reads 43 degrees Celsius. Strangely **LUTHER** looks cold and ill. He turns the car fan onto full heat and air thrust. He smiles and puts one hand right up close to the grill. He moves his face closer to enjoy the heat more too.

He is distracted when he sees a little gas station ahead, which we know is **HARRY'S** garage.

Camera stays at the garage level and looks past the pumps and watches **LUTHER** drive off towards the town-ship a mile or two on from the garage. We hold this shot, another car pulls into **HARRY'S** garage.

We see this from the POV of the road looking on. **HARRY** steps out of the kiosk building towelling his hands down with a greasy rag, he walks up to attend the car.

HARRY nods to the man inside the car and walks round to the nozzle and starts to fill it up. The man in the car rolls down his window.

MAN
Good day Sir.

HARRY
Good day.

JUMP CUT TO:

24 EXT. HARRY'S GARAGE FORE COURT. DUSK. 24

HARRY and the customer walk across the fore court to the kiosk building.

CUT TO:

25 EXT. NEVADA TOWN-SHIP. DUSK. 25

LUTHER drives past a sign that is home-made and says: "Welcome to Sunburn". He drives through the strange little town. A few people glance briefly at him. This is a very tired and weary little town. **LUTHER'S** stomach rumbles. He sees a little bar/diner on one of the little street corners.

(CONTINUED)

25 CONTINUED: 25

A big green neon sign reading "Fat Mans' hangs outside the diner. **LUTHER** parks his truck on the side of the road outside "Fat Mans'". **LUTHER** gets out, and takes in the night for a few moments.

A massive muscled tall man walks past him and glances at him momentarily and then moves on. **LUTHER** is surprised at the size of him.

LUTHER walks along the street to the diner, the colored and lit windows and shop fronts illuminating **LUTHER** in the most amazing colors. **LUTHER** gets to the diner.

He walks in, the bell above the door tinkles. The people inside, bearded, tough and grizzled double take as they don't recognise him. They look at him for a bit too long, making him uncomfortable. **LUTHER**, sensing this, gives a small toothless smile. The customers look away and go back to their business after that.

The floor is very worn and faded checker-board pattern, with perishing holey linoleum.

One man still looks at **LUTHER**, a thick and milky trail of smoke defies gravity and cascades up round his face.

LUTHER sits at a little two-seater table. He reads the menu. He looks at all the options, mostly steaks and grilled meat. **LUTHER** waves over a waitress.

LUTHER
Hey, could I get a big burger, with a glass of water and a whiskey, with no ice please.

We don't know this is **NANCY** yet.

NANCY
(Joking slightly.)
Neat!...Sure thing hon, commin' right up.

LUTHER yawns deeply and massages his face with his hands. He looks out the dusty plate-glass windows to look upon the dark dusty street.

LUTHER walks up to a news paper rack and runs his finger to the top. The most recent paper is two years old.

(CONTINUED)

25 CONTINUED: (2) 25

He rolls his eyes and takes it back to his table. He reads it. There are pages of adds and local and mining news. He flips over a few more pages, and he sees a certain article.

The paper has a picture of a dead body. The paper reads: Doctors and experts are left clueless as man violently dies through causes unknown. Man (pictured) was in local diner when stated to gag on his frozen yoghurt-

LUTHER gets a slight jump when **NANCY** arrives at his table with his food. The glass of water overflows slightly.

LUTHER
Thanks.

She walks away. **LUTHER** checks out her butt clad in a tight short skirt and her perfect smooth symmetrical legs as she walks away.

26 TIME LAPSE: INT. FAT MAN'S DINER. NIGHT. 26

Close on: **LUTHER'S** burger, slowly starts to become a ghost burger with bites out of it and become more and more transparent, until it is completely gone. **LUTHER** finishes his last swig of whisky as well.

NANCY
(Seeing this.)
Hey there, let me get ya' a fresh one sport.

LUTHER
Thanks.

NANCY carries his drink over.

LUTHER
(Looking at her.)
Thanks.

The two muscle men at the other end of the diner study **LUTHER** and **NANCY** whilst they eat their meat.

NANCY
I ain't seen you 'fore round here.

LUTHER
I'm from outta town.

(CONTINUED)

26 CONTINUED: 26

NANCY
You can say that again trooper!

NANCY winks and walks off back behind the bar.

LUTHER goes to reach for his paper again, but sees it has been taken away. He looks a bit annoyed at that. There's a commotion and shouting coming from the kitchen. The tenants in the diner look round idly.

The two muscle men in the diner still have their gaze fixed on **LUTHER** and seem to ignore this new commotion.

NANCY charges out shortly followed by a fat and greasy **COOK** holding a meat cleaver. **NANCY** takes off her apron and throws it at the **COOK.**

NANCY
You can take your job and shove it up your inaccessibly fat ass! You fat fuck!

COOK
Get your useless stinky, sweaty, sticky, slutty cunt outta ma' restaurant ya'dumb bitch!

The fat **COOK** waddles back into the kitchen mumbling:

COOK
Cunt.

NANCY storms out the diner, some customers look at her bum on her way out. **LUTHER** on the other hand is quite shocked. He gets up and leaves. The tenants pay no heed whatsoever to **LUTHER'S** departure, apart from the ones who are watching **LUTHER.**

27 EXT. NEVADA TOWNSHIP. NIGHT. 27

NANCY stands on the street corner. An orange dust blows through on a night zephyr. Some sleepy electronic music plays. Little cars and pick-ups trundle through the street. **NANCY** stands looking downcast and hurt shivering slightly. A little tumble-weed blows along the street. **NANCY** takes out a pack of cigarette and holds it up to her mouth, pulling a cigarette out with her teeth. She pulls out a lighter. Close on: lighter with a snake engraving on it. She lights up, wispy smoke blows around.

(CONTINUED)

27 CONTINUED: 27

LUTHER walks out a bit cold, with his hands in his pocket, he looks concerned and outraged. **LUTHER** sees she is smoking.

LUTHER
(Pointing to cigarete.)
A gun would be faster and easier.

NANCY turns round, smiles slightly.

NANCY
Assumin' that fat fuck doesn't do the honours first.

LUTHER chuckles. **NANCY** drops the cigarette after one last drag.

LUTHER
Some would say that's a great waste of tobacco. You can't win can you?

NANCY
That's my life.

LUTHER
Don't worry... you can believe me, I've been there.

NANCY
(Thinks for a moment.)
Really?

LUTHER
Yeah... I don't know a time when life wasn't trying to kill me.

Both laugh. **LUTHER** looks a bit more sincere.

LUTHER
Look, I'm really sorry about what happened in there.

NANCY
(Caring.)
But that wasn't your fault.

LUTHER
I know, but... it's quite embarrassing when these things happen.

27 CONTINUED: (2) 27

NANCY
Very!

LUTHER
Yeah, very. Are you sure you're alright?

NANCY
Oh yeah, something will turn up, something always does... My uncle Harry will be picking me up in a half hour.

LUTHER
Do you wanna lift?

NANCY
Oh, no it's ok, you don't have to.

LUTHER
Come on, I insist. And don't worry I'm not a "Strange" man, although I'm sure that's exactly what strange men would say.

NANCY smiles and shakes a little in the cold. They walk towards **LUTHER'S** truck.

LUTHER
(Put's hand out.)
I'm Luther...Luther Teller.

NANCY
(Put's her hand out.)
I'm Nancy. I, uh, don't really have a second name.

LUTHER
What? You don't have a second name?

NANCY
Nope, I'm Nancy and ma uncles Harry, and that's the way it's always bin'.

LUTHER thinks a moment, smiles and gets in his car. Camera then sees a shot of the car mirror. We see, through a dusty glaze the town with the diner fade into the distance, camera tracks back revealing this whole shot was being seen as a refection in the wing mirror.

28 INT. LUTHER'S CAR. NEVADA DESERT. NIGHT. 28

NANCY lies back, tired in the car seat. She stretches her legs as far as they will go. **LUTHER** peers over slightly to take another look at her. They sit in silence for a few moments. They glance at each other waiting for some inspiration to initiate a conversation.

LUTHER squirms around a little, he turns and opens his mouth to say something, but then doesn't and returns to his first position. **NANCY** noticing this giggles.

NANCY
So... where might you be from...Luther?

LUTHER
(Smiles slightly.)
I, uh... well it's actually a harder question to answer than you might think. I was born and raised in Detroit, but we're not from there.

NANCY
Where are you from?

LUTHER
My parents said,... uh, that I'm actually from somewhere around here originally... I think... Where are you from?

NANCY looks a little perturbed and tries to conceal this.

NANCY
Born and bred!

LUTHER
You said, your uncle Harry?

NANCY
Yeah, my mommy died in childbirth and my daddy, he uh, well we don't know where he is, I never seen him. And my uncle Harry, he's the best guy in the world! You can't beat uncle Harry, he raised me y'know, all my life as if I was his own, as well as runnin' two businesses, the station and the crematorium.

28 CONTINUED: 28

LUTHER
Crematorium?

NANCY
Yeah, there ain't no one else is there, not in a town like this.

LUTHER
Sounds like an upstanding guy, better than lots of other's. My dad, he loved his work really more than anything, I didn't really know him at all until I was 15 or so. Bit of an indifferent jerk really.

NANCY
That sucks man!

LUTHER
Nah it's alright, nothin' lost nothin' gained y'know.

NANCY
I know what you mean, I mean I've never left this valley in my life.

LUTHER
What! You serious?

NANCY
Is that a bad thing?

LUTHER
Uh, no, but, it's just a surprise. Do you ever go on holiday or anythin'?

NANCY
Uh, well, uh...

LUTHER can see he's put her on the spot, so he changes the subject.

LUTHER
No matter anyway, do you want the heat up? It's getting quite cold.

NANCY
Oh, yes please!

LUTHER puts the fan and heat up to their top registers. He exhales and looks like he has just sexually climaxed when he puts one of his hands next to one of the heat grills.

(CONTINUED)

28 CONTINUED: (2) 28

NANCY notices this and frowns thinking, she turns to the front with a bit of a shock. We see this potent reaction.

NANCY
So what brings you out here then partner?

LUTHER
Well uh, uh,...

NANCY sees she's put him on the spot, but she wants to know so encourages him.

NANCY
I'm sorry, I didn't mean to-

LUTHER
Oh no it's ok, 'bout time I said it all anyway... I, uh, well my parents passed away a year ago-

NANCY
I'm sorry to hear that.

LUTHER
Thanks, it's ok though, it was nice in the end for them anyway.

NANCY
D'ya mind sayin' how they...

LUTHER
It was cancer.

NANCY
Oh, no!

LUTHER
Well, these things happen eh? And...

NANCY looks intrigued.

LUTHER
And, I myself have just recovered from cancer.

NANCY
(Shocked and surprised.)
WHAT!? But you're so young.

LUTHER
Yeah, I know, but no one knows what it was, I mean me and my folks all had the same type, it wasn't like it was one kind in one person and another in another, it was all the same, and cancer isn't infectious, and no one knew what the hell it was.

NANCY tries to conceal her great shock and wondering.

LUTHER
It just seemed to be everywhere, but no-where at the same time, they couldn't find a primary and it finished my folks off pretty quick, but I just recovered, just got over it, I was on deaths door one minute and up and about the next, I don't know, what the hell it was about, all the oncologists and medical professionals were clueless...it was just insane.

NANCY'S eyes widen, and she looks increasingly worried, she smiles and **LUTHER.** She puts her chin in her hand and gazes out the window to hide her surprise.

LUTHER
So I'm just trying to find out what the hell happened, and I reckoned, there's got to be something here, y'know, answers or the like, this was where they were born y'know? You got any friends round here?

NANCY wakes up a bit from this.

NANCY
Uh, oh yeah! There's some great gals here, their's Belinda Ennis, and uh, Andy Walker...ah, whatamma sayin' you don't know these gals...oh and there's also Mike! Old Ivy's funny too.

LUTHER
(Luther smiles, mystified.)
I'm sorry, Ivy?

28 CONTINUED: (4) 28

NANCY gets a jolt of adrenaline as she realizes she may have let something slip. **LUTHER** doesn't notice this.

NANCY
Oh, what?

LUTHER
You said "Old Ivy's funny", what's Ivy?

NANCY
Did I say that now? Oh Luther, the tiredness must be git'n to me.

LUTHER
Speaking of tiredness-

NANCY looks very relieved as **LUTHER** hasn't picked up on it any more and that she dodged a bullet there.

LUTHER
-I have this dream, where I'm crawling round a room,-

NANCY looks very frightened and worried when she hears this and again, does her best to hide it.

LUTHER
Is this the place?

NANCY
What? Is what what place?

LUTHER
Is this where you stay?

NANCY
(Looks out the window.)
Oh, yeah, sorry Luth, I need to get to bed.

LUTHER
Yeah, me too. Where would you recommend in town?

NANCY
Oh, uh, I'd recommend Bravo's. We like to call it "The Castle" in town.

They laugh. **LUTHER** drives into the garage and past some petrol pumps up to the door. There's a light on inside. **HARRY** can be seen inside in the distance in overalls.

(CONTINUED)

NANCY
Thank you very much Luther... feel free to pull a little petrol for your time.

LUTHER
Oh, no it was my pleasure, forget it!

NANCY
Thanks very much Luther, you're real kind.

LUTHER nods in acknowledgement.

NANCY smiles and shuts the door. She walks up towards the garage. **LUTHER** watches her and thinks for a moment. He scrambles out the car.

LUTHER
(Calling out.)
Hey!

NANCY turns.

LUTHER
Would you like to... I dunno, go for a drink tomorrow?

NANCY smiles.

NANCY
Yeah, I would really like that. How about "Tritium's" on the main-street at 12:00?

LUTHER smiles and looks very happy.

LUTHER
That's perfect.

NANCY
See ya then partner!

NANCY winks and walks inside. **LUTHER** sits in his car smiling to himself.

LUTHER reverses out the garage and drives back down the track towards the town.

28 CONTINUED: (6) 28

Camera ascends up to a small Ariel shot. A dusty trail accompanies the car into the night.

TRANSITION TO:

29 EXT. NEVADA TOWNSHIP. NIGHT. OUTSIDE BRAVO'S. 29

Bravo's is a large motel, with a kind of alamo style front. It has (Bravo's) written on the front, in weathered imprint, i.e. shots are seen of Bravo's.

Luther's truck trundles down the dusty street. It pulls down a little side alley, where a sign points (Parking). He pulls up next to another worn but larger 4X4 truck.

TRANSITION TO:

30 INT. BRAVO'S MOTEL. NIGHT. 30

LUTHER walks along the dusty out-door balcony to his room past a sign that reads: (Conseeerj). **LUTHER** shakes his head and tuts at this.

TRANSITION TO:

31 INT. BRAVO MOTEL ROOM. NIGHT. 31

We see drawer handles jagging into the shot from one side. Two hands pull the drawers they are attached to out and places some clothing into them.

LUTHER pauses and looks at the lamp on his bed-side table (which is turned on). He rests his suit case down on the bed. He sits down. He continues to study his lamp.

His face displays a strange kind of longing. His mouth is open slightly, making little jerky movements.

He slowly reaches over and removes the lamp-shade. Slowly and sensually he slides his mouth over the light bulb illuminating his face flesh bright yellow and red, light even comes out of his nostrils. He groans in pleasure. He stays here for a while, camera watches him for a while.

He takes his mouth off of the bulb, and looks around nervously, wondering what the hell is going on.

(CONTINUED)

31 CONTINUED: 31

He is soon distracted by another thought, he looks towards his bathroom.

LUTHER strips off and stands in the shower.

He pulls the red hot lever down fully. He groans a little as the scorching water cascades down over him. He grits his teeth and grunts as he settles into it. Steam billows out of the shower. He stands there in strange enjoyment, looking up, to let it drench his face.

FADE TO BLACK:

32 EXT. BRAVO MOTEL. MORNING. 32

LUTHER exits his room. He walks along the balcony past all the rooms, which are all empty. He passes one of the muscle men from the diner. **LUTHER** displays a look of slight recognition.

33 INT. CAFE. MORNING. 33

On entrance **LUTHER** realizes he is the only person there. A weather-beaten old-timer stands behind the counter. **LUTHER** gazes around the place on his way to the counter, we see what he sees.

OLD TIMER
What'll it be mister?

LUTHER
Uh, could I please have a stack of pancakes with syrup please?

OLD TIMER
Comin' up.

LUTHER
Thanks.

34 EXT. STREET. MORNING. 34

LUTHER walks out of the diner and down the street wiping his mouth. He sits on a worn little bench in the street.

DISSOLVE TO:

35 EXT. STREET, A BIT LATER. DAY. 35

It is a scorching morning, probably about 43 degrees celsius. **LUTHER** walks down the street and is met with a few looks from people on his way.

36 EXT. DIFFERENT TOWNSHIP STREET. DAY. 36

LUTHER walks down a more residential looking street with small scruffy terraced sort of buildings. He walks up to a property.

JUMP CUT TO:

37 EXT. OUTSIDE WOMAN'S HOUSE. DAY. 37

A middle-aged townswoman answers.

WOMAN
Help you mister?

LUTHER
Uh, actually yes... see I'm new in town, and I was just wondering if I could ask you a few questions...

At this the **WOMAN** seizes up.

WOMAN
I can't help you I'm sorry...

LUTHER takes a few steps forward.

LUTHER
But-...

The **WOMAN** shuts the door on him. **LUTHER** flaps his arms up and then down in exasperation.

LUTHER walks to another house.

A man opens the door, and sticks the shot-gun in **LUTHER'S** face, **LUTHER** gets a bit of a fright at this. But then the **MAN** lowers it.

MAN
What can I do for ya'mister?

(CONTINUED)

37 CONTINUED: 37

LUTHER
I- I'm new in town see, and, I believe that my family lived here a number of years ago.

MAN
What's your name?

LUTHER
Luther, sir Luther Teller.

The man shakes his head.

MAN
Nope, doesn't ring any bells.

LUTHER
Are you sure?

MAN
Born and bred, I think I would know a thing or two about the town.

LUTHER
Thank you for your trouble.

The **MAN** shuts the door and **LUTHER** walks away shaking his head, he is feeling strange vibes and looks completely bewildered.

In the distance one of the muscle-men drive past. **LUTHER** doesn't see.

Montage of: **LUTHER** being turned away from a number of different houses.

He pauses at the end of the street, thinking and confused. A strange man stands at the street corner. He stares at **LUTHER. LUTHER** looks round uncomfortably. He nods to the man and continues on his way. The man continues to look at him.

Camera sees **LUTHER'S** uncomfortable face from the front.

LUTHER walks up to the last house in the street.

38 EXT. GERRY LEE'S HOUSE. DAY. 38

The house looks deserted, but isn't. An **OLDER WOMAN** rocks on a chair with a book in her hand in the window. **LUTHER** walks up to her house and knocks.

A voice can be heard from inside.

VOICE
Ahh!! I'm comin'!!! I ain't got the strength I used to!

An **OLDER WOMAN** who looks like a strangely cool, but still a scruffy version of the traditional desert dweller in dungarees opens the door. Pointing a six shot revolver pistol at **LUTHER. LUTHER** flinches.

GERRY LEE
I'm sorry mister, force a' habit.

GERRY LEE lowers the pistol.

LUTHER
Hello, I'm new in town, and I wondered if you could spare a few moments to answer a few questions?

GERRY LEE
(Rough booming voice.)
COME INSIDE!!!

GERRY LEE ushers **LUTHER** in zealously. We feel she is glad of the rare occurrence of human company.

The house is dilapidated with no curtains, a radio on a chair, and boards on the ground.

GERRY LEE
Siddan'!! Siddan'! Ma man, and I'll git' ya a beer!

LUTHER
Thanks, you're very kind.

GERRY LEE limps slightly to a cooler in the kitchen, and throws a beer across the room. **LUTHER** catches it (only just). **LUTHER** gingerly opens it. He takes a refreshing swig out of it.

LUTHER
Delicious beer ma'am.

GERRY LEE
Ah, it's a gid brew it's a gid brew! So, whit' brings you ta this neck of the woods mister?

LUTHER
Well I uh, my parents passed away-

GERRY LEE
I's sorry to here that mister!

LUTHER
Thank you, but uh, they told me, that our family was originally from this town, a while back and I just wanted to see if I could find some answers.

GERRY LEE
What's yir name sir?

LUTHER
Teller, ma'am.

GERRY LEE
(Thinks.)
Teller, Teller... doesn't ring any bells. I useda live in the other valley until about 15 years ago, and they cleared out ma hometown for the Provin' Grounds and weapons testin' and what not. We was very angry 'bout it. With all the desert out there and they have to clear our tiny lousy little patch out.

LUTHER nods in understanding.

LUTHER
I understand completely ma'am.

GERRY LEE
But if you goes along and see Doctor Oppenheimer, he'll have all the medical records of everywin' from at least the war!

LUTHER
I shall do just that ma'am.

GERRY LEE
D'ya wanna see somethin' weird?

(CONTINUED)

38 CONTINUED: (2) 38

LUTHER
Okay?

GERRY LEE brings a bag of dust from under her seat and tosses it to **LUTHER.**

GERRY LEE
Take a look in that bag!

LUTHER does.

LUTHER
It...it's ash?

GERRY LEE
Ash with bones in it!

LUTHER picks up a little lump in the ash, it has a bone fragment in it.

LUTHER
Oh my GOD!

GERRY LEE
There's piles of the stuff all around this town here, I dunno where they put it, but the wind piles it up in ma' back yard. I've found all sirtsa bone and shit init! And I know it ain't the crematorium, they give the ashes back ta the families see, so no ash gits outside.

LUTHER
Yes I was gonna ask about the crematorium. What direction does the wind come from to blow it into your back-yard?

GERRY LEE
North, I think.

LUTHER
Well are there any developments or anything to the north.

GERRY LEE
Not that I can see.

LUTHER
You said they? Who's they?

(CONTINUED)

38 CONTINUED: (3) 38

GERRY LEE
I don't know, but word spreads in this town, and ya' just don't speak about others to others, but I don't know shit about anything, so I dunno whit' they're all talkin' 'bout and that's how I want to keep it.

LUTHER looks very puzzled.

GERRY LEE
But if ya'ask me mister, I min' like if ah had a gun ta' ma head and I had ta' give an answer like, then... I'd say it all has somethin' ta do wi' these bombs. These fuckin' bombs! We were never meant ta' put that power through the ground. The mining is bad an' damagin' enough without these sons a' bitches. Did you know mister these irresponsible assholes are thinkin' a' usin' fuckin' atomic bombs fur minin'! They say it'll "effectively loosen the ground", yeah no shit genius!

LUTHER
Jesus Christ! They aren't are they?

GERRY LEE
Ya' bet yur ass mister. Yeah, I think there's some sorta, I ah dunno, conspiracy or some shit, so many of these morons get too close to the tests ya' know, I mean these imbeciles are getting up to the megaton magnitude and their viewin' the tests from three kilometers away, get the hell outta' here, these idiots need to try timsing that by a hundred at least, to make sure they get outta' that fall out cloud too! No wonder these suckers are being fuckin' vaporized as near as that to the tests, serves them right as far as I'm concerned!

LUTHER
Absolutely ma'am!

(CONTINUED)

38 CONTINUED: (4) 38

GERRY LEE
Anyway mister, even if it ain't the bombs vaporisin' people... somethin's vaporisin' people out here!

LUTHER thinks, looking at **GERRY LEE**, mystified and worried.

GERRY LEE
D'ya know what the roaring sound is after these bombs detonate? First off, I can tell ya' it's not God or Satan bellowin' out from the abyss... no!

GERRY LEE demonstrates with a hand movement quickly shaking her hand vertically up and down.

GERRY LEE
It's the shock waves bouncin' back and forth between the earth and the o-zone layer millions, yes literally fuckin' millions of times a second... I think the blast propels the sound waves faster than usual... Y'know mister they told me it was going to be like a Polaroid snap... but it wasn't! (Chuckles), it certainly was not.

GERRY LEE looks to **LUTHER.**

GERRY LEE
Well how the hell could it be? Equivalent of a quarter of a million tons of Tri-Nitro Toluene. That's how they measure these suckers now, in kilo tons and mega tons if ya' can believe it, yes "equivalent to the explosion of so many tons of TNT" that's what these idiots say. Yes, 250 Kilotons, that's what it was!

LUTHER
Well, uh, I've taken up enough of your time ma'am, but thank you very much for it.

(CONTINUED)

GERRY LEE
(Wearily.)
Not at all mister, I'm goin' for a knap, but ya drop in agin' if ya have yoursilf iny more questions. And ah mean thit, hold me to it if ya don't believe me.

LUTHER
I will, thank you and I do believe you ma'am.

GERRY LEE
If y'ask me mister, Ida thought yer folks didn't tell ya 'bout this place for a reason.

LUTHER goes to walk out but stops.

GERRY LEE sees this.

GERRY LEE
Is somethin' on your mind mister?

LUTHER
(Gestures.)
Yeah, a man outside is just standing on the street corner and he just stood there staring at me.

GERRY LEE chuckles.

LUTHER, relived nods.

LUTHER sees himself out. He stands out on the dusty track very puzzled.

LUTHER
(To himself)
Ash with bones in it.

LUTHER looks up into the pristine blue sky and the scorching sun. He baths his face in its raw rays. He relaxes massively when his face is in the sun.

LUTHER looks at his watch. It reads 11:47. **LUTHER'S** eyes swell when he realizes how close the time is. He rushes along the street.

39 INT. GERRY LEE'S HOUSE. DAY. 39

We are back in **GERRY LEE'S** house. He sleeps on a very rickety frame of a bed. There is a banging knock coming from the back door.

Gerry LEE wakes with a start, and mumbles and grumbles in annoyance. The knocking intensifies and continues.

GERRY LEE
I'm comin', I'm comin' hold yar horses feller!

GERRY LEE stands up and starts to limp towards the door. But he stops as the knocking becomes thunderous and relentless. He doesn't like this. He stops speaking. He looks worried and serious. He quietly makes his way to the door. He reaches above the door and takes the six shot revolver pistol down, cocks it and holds it up.

When Gerry **LEE** gets to the back door, he opens it and thrusts the pistol in the face of his visitor.

GERRY LEE looks on in terror.

DOMINIC SUNSET stands there in blue mechanic overalls, gas mask and what looks like a D.I.Y flame-thrower. The thrower, is like a large rectangular bicycle pump, with two handles protruding, a coiled metal pipe leads from a tank on his back into the thrower.

The mechanism is designed to pump streams of flammable liquid past a constantly lit pilot light, which is attached to the bottom of the nozzle where the stream would come from.

DOMINIC SUNSET boots Gerry **LEE** back to the ground. **DOMINIC SUNSET** aims the thrower and Gerry **LEE** whips up his arm and shoots at **DOMINIC SUNSET**, a shot tears through **DOMINIC SUNSET'S** shoulder and he lets out a choked bellow of pain through the gas mask. Gerry **LEE** goes to fire again aiming at **DOMINIC SUNSET'S** face. **DOMINIC SUNSET** is too quick and with brutal force kicks the gun out of Gerry **LEE'S** hand, the gun goes off again.

39 CONTINUED: 39

GERRY LEE scrambles to his feet and takes a piece of protruding wood from his wall and breaks it off and smashes it repeatedly off the side of **DOMINIC SUNSET'S** head, Sunset groans in pain at this. **DOMINIC SUNSET** manages to catch it stopping Gerry **LEE** from striking again. But, Gerry **LEE** releases one of his hands and picks up a lamp from a nearby table and clobbers **DOMINIC SUNSET'S** head with it, blood seeps through the fabric of **DOMINIC SUNSET'S** gas mask. **DOMINIC SUNSET** boots **GERRY LEE** down again.

DOMINIC SUNSET is far too fast and strong. He pumps the make shift flame thrower with a metal handle, spraying Gerry **LEE** with a stream of fire, Gerry **LEE** collapses bellowing and thrashing around in pain.

DOMINIC SUNSET strides over Gerry **LEE** and proceeds to set Gerry Lee's house on fire.

40 INT. NEVADA TOWNSHIP. BAR. DAY. 40

NANCY sits on a tall nimble bar-stool. She wears some cool narrow wool-mix drapy trousers and a pleated blouse with big shoulder pads. She sits there gazing over to the up-turned bottles behind the bar-counter. Some people are puffing away on roll ups and fags by the windows, so there is a smoky and hazy atmosphere in the bar, the glass in the windows is a little distorted so there is a very blue and green sort of glow in the joint. A lot of men smoke outside so there is a further miasma of smoke at the windows on the outside.

LUTHER bursts in, in dark trousers, a cement colored stand-up nero-collared shirt and a dark long jacket. He looks at a clock on the wall and it's 12:04. **LUTHER** spots **NANCY** and walks over to her. She hasn't noticed **LUTHER,** he is quite glad and composes himself before walking up to her. His face calms when he sees her, the ash with the bones in it is at the back of his mind here. Music plays in the bar.

LUTHER
(With a dry smile.)
Hi there.

NANCY turns round, with a cheeky smile.

NANCY
Hi there to you to darlin'.

(CONTINUED)

40 CONTINUED: 40

LUTHER smiles and takes a seat.

LUTHER
What'll you be having?

NANCY
I think I'll see off a breakfast cocktail.

LUTHER
Good choice... I've never had one before but good choice.

They laugh.

LUTHER
(Waves to barman.)
Could I have a breakfast Martini for the lady and a scotch neat.

The bar man nods his head.

NANCY
What are you Luther? I mean, what do ya' do?

LUTHER
I, uh, well I tried to teach in Saskatchewan.

NANCY
Sorry?

LUTHER
Canada.

NANCY nods her head. The waitress brings their drinks over. **NANCY** obviously knows her and smiles to her. And the waitress smiles back to **NANCY**.

LUTHER
But I sucked at that, so I drove around a bit looking for some training of some kind, but nothing showed up, and then I got a call telling me about the passing of... my grandparents. Then a few years later my parents. I had been in between things in those two years, trying to help them along, but I ended up couch-surfing and doing manual labour, because my folks had to sell their house to help with the care.

(CONTINUED)

NANCY
(A bit on edge.)
So, uh, d'ya think y'all stay long here?

LUTHER
I dunno,... I really don't know anything anymore... but anyway, onto better things eh?

NANCY
Yeah, I could see you as a sorta, shrink person... like a counsellor or somethin'.

LUTHER
Really? Well I think you would be a real good... model.

NANCY blushes a little.

LUTHER
But I think you need a break first. Something tells me it's not been easy for you.

All the people who were smoking from outside come in. They draw the blinds and lock the door.

NANCY turns round and sees this.

NANCY
Put your hand over your drink.

LUTHER baffled does so. The whole place shakes a bit and a distant rumble is heard and the liquid in their drinks sloshes.

LUTHER
What the hell is that? An earthquake?

NANCY
(Quite casually.)
Nah, just another test, they'll probably give it an hour before going back out again.

LUTHER
Sure.

40 CONTINUED: (3) 40

NANCY
Anyway...Well I suppose I have had a tough time in a way, I mean, I help Uncle Harry out with the garage and the cleaning and maintenance of stuff, it's hard work.

LUTHER
D'ya think you might go to school somewhere?

NANCY
(On edge again.)
I-I did think about going to V-Vegas or Pheonix and learnin' some sorta work on the tables, y'know. But Uncle Harry would be all alone without me.

LUTHER
He's a mature man, he would manage surely.

NANCY
(Getting a bit uncomfortable.)
I-I I'm sure he would be okay, it's just that- He's been so good to me.

LUTHER
I'm sorry, I don't mean to-

NANCY
- Luther... i-i- it's more than... than just that y'see...y'see I can't leave, I start to get ill if I try.

LUTHER
Don't worry, everybody gets home-sick.

NANCY smiles, but is a little annoyed, it's not what she meant.

NANCY
(She laughs.)
Oh Luther, you are funny, you have these kind of Lutherisms.

LUTHER
Like what?

(CONTINUED)

40 CONTINUED: (4) 40

NANCY
You have this thing about people, you seem to want to find out all you can about people.

LUTHER
I guess I am very interested in what and who I don't understand.

NANCY
Do you not understand me?

LUTHER
Not entirely, but I'm getting there... I think.

They smile dryly at each other. **LUTHER** catches sight of a small thermometer hanging with her keys and compact make up unit. He wonders at this. He is about to ask when;

NANCY
I think a person can't understand everything about their life though.

LUTHER
I could not agree more. After this cancer shit in my life, I think I was meant to bump into a very beautiful girl in a Nevada diner.

NANCY is very touched by this. But also troubled by it as well. **LUTHER** kind of notices this, not understanding wanting to know why, hence his questioning.

NANCY
(Pulling back.)
Life isn't about livin' and dyin', it's everything in between.

41 EXT. NEVADA TOWNSHIP. DAY. 41

In street out side the old Man's house.

A man **WARREN** (40s) with stubble and scruffy desert clothing with a few concerned towns-people are all crowded out-side the old Man's house. **WARREN** walks slowly up to the house. The house has blackened windows.

41 CONTINUED: 41

WARREN
Gerry Lee! Gerry Lee! Are you ok, old woman? Are ya' there Gerry Lee?

WOMAN
Maybe she's passed away?

WARREN
(To Woman.)
I'll go check if she's okay.

WARREN pulls out a large hunting knife. He walks up to the door.

42 INT. TRITIUMS. TOWNSHIP. DAY. 42

LUTHER and **NANCY** get up to leave.

LUTHER
There is something that is puzzling me though.

NANCY
What's that?

LUTHER
This mornin' I was asking round town to see if anyone knew my folks, but none of 'em had a clue. And I don't understand how people who have lived here for generations wouldn't have at least heard of my parents.

NANCY
Maybe this ain't the right valley.

LUTHER
Well are there any other valley's near this one?

NANCY
(Almost says something else.)
Yeah, I suppose.

LUTHER
Anyway I spoke to this one old fella, and he had a bag of ash... that had bones in it.

42 CONTINUED: 42

NANCY has her back to **LUTHER** as she picks up her hand-bag. She looks very worried for a moment.

NANCY
M-maybe it was him, y'know how crazy some old folks can be.

LUTHER
Yeah, but he said that the wind blew piles of it into his back yard. I think something's going on, and I think that maybe your uncle Harry might be able to help me.

NANCY
(Nervously.)
Yeah he might.

43 EXT. OUTSIDE OLD MANS HOUSE. DAY. 43

WARREN walks up to Gerry Lees' door. He knocks. He knocks again.

WARREN
Gerry LEE!!!???

WARREN hears yelling from the people who went round the back. He barges in and goes to see. He yelps and falls back in shock at seeing the charred remains of **GERRY LEE. WARREN** holds his sleeve up to his nose and cringes in disgust at the sight.

44 INT. LUTHER'S TRUCK. DAY. 44

LUTHER and **NANCY** sit in silence. They both know the other knows something and find it difficult to speak knowing this about each other. They occasionally smile at each other; trying to reassure each other there is no palpable tension in the car, when they know there is.

DISSOLVE TO:

45 EXT. HARRY'S GARAGE. DAY. 45

LUTHER'S truck pulls up to a pump in Harry's garage.

HARRY emerges out of the kiosk house in dirty mechanic overalls. He wipes down his hands with a rag.

(CONTINUED)

45 CONTINUED: 45

An **ASSISTANT** in similar clothing as **HARRY** runs out too and starts to polish the cosmetic work of Luther's car. **HARRY** fiddles with and rattles his rattle. His stony and almost bored face looking at **LUTHER. NANCY** hesitates for a second and then makes the introductions.

NANCY
Luther, this is my uncle Harry.

HARRY'S eyes widen slightly and he walks towards **LUTHER. HARRY** puts on a small toothless smile. They shake hands.

LUTHER
It's a pleasure to meet you sir.

HARRY
Pleasure.

LUTHER
Your niece has told me a good deal about you.

HARRY
Yes, where is it you're from?

LUTHER
I was born in Detroit, but I think I'm originally from here.

HARRY
Yeah? What's your family name?

LUTHER
Teller, sir.

HARRY
(Shakes head.)
Can't say I've heard of it.

LUTHER
Yeah, I've been all around town inquiring, but no one seems to know about them, I'm beginning to think I might I have come to the wrong valley.

HARRY
Yeah.

LUTHER notices a metal chamber buried with rubbish at the rear of the garage. **HARRY** sees this.

LUTHER
Is that you're crematorium?

HARRY
Yeah.

HARRY takes a small thermometer out of his pocket, looks at it and then puts it away again. **LUTHER** notices and wonders at this, we see it in his face. The **ASSISTANT** looks to **LUTHER** in a some what worried way. **LUTHER** nervously smiles at him. The **ASSISTANT** scuttles off.

LUTHER
(Making
conversation.)
When did you get this place?

HARRY
What does it matter?

LUTHER is a little dented by this remark.

LUTHER
No, I just.

HARRY
(Very calmly.)
You just what?

HARRY looks at **LUTHER** with a completely still and calm face.

LUTHER
I-I was just wondering.

LUTHER looks round to **NANCY**, who is involved with her make up compact.

LUTHER
T-there was something I thought
you could help me with sir.

HARRY remains silent.

LUTHER feels another thing fall upon silence. **LUTHER** is distracted by the fact that he notices that **HARRY** and **NANCY** are not sweating at all and he is pouring. He discreetly looks at his soaking sweaty shirt.

45 CONTINUED: (3) 45

LUTHER
This morning I visited a resident, who had lived in the town for 15 years, and he had reported piles of ash in his back yard, ash that had bones in it. Since you live and work here, surely you must see all the comings and goings of the town. Have you seen anything strange?

HARRY just screws his mouth up and shakes his head.

LUTHER
He said the ash was blowing in from the north, but the north is just open desert, ash of that quantity would need to come from an inhabited area.

HARRY
Yes it would. But as you can see we do not have any trees in the area, so ash is very unlikely to form.

LUTHER can't but agree.

LUTHER
Sir, the residents don't care to say much.

HARRY just shakes his head again.

LUTHER
Well thank you very much for your help sir, but I'd best be going. I've got a doctors appointment in an hour.

HARRY takes very strong yet subtle notice of this.

LUTHER receives no response from **HARRY** for this either. **HARRY** just stands there blankly. **LUTHER** makes some half smiles and mumbles gingerly as he goes back to his car.

LUTHER
Bye Nancy.

45 CONTINUED: (4) 45

NANCY
(Containing nervousness.)
Bye Luther.

LUTHER is very mystified. He drives off not looking back.

46 INT. LUTHER'S CAR. DAY. 46

As **LUTHER** gets about 200 feet away from the garage he sees the **ASSISTANT** running after him. Wondering if the Assistant thinks he perhaps forgot something he pulls over.

47 EXT. DESERT ROAD. DAY. 47

LUTHER gets out of the car. **LUTHER** starts to back away seeing this man running at him. The **ASSISTANT** sinks to his knees and grabs **LUTHER'S** shirt.

ASSISTANT
Luther, help me!

The two of them look round as **HARRY** approaches. The **ASSISTANT** gets up and runs back. **HARRY** looks at **LUTHER.**

HARRY
(Points to his head.)
Sorry about that, he has... issues.

LUTHER smiles and nods trying to conceal his worry. He gets back in his car and drives off without looking back. **HARRY** looks on after him for a beat and then looks back to the station, his face inscrutable.

48 EXT. HARRY'S GARAGE. DAY. 48

HARRY keeps looking at Luther's car driving off into the distance. He turns round to a very worried looking **NANCY.** His facial expression is very strange. It's the lack of any real expression that is perturbing **NANCY** so much. **HARRY** holds his gaze on her for a bit too long too. He takes a walkie-talkie out of his overalls and walks away and talks into it as he goes.

48 CONTINUED: 48

NANCY looks very worried looking at **HARRY** walk back to the kiosk building.

49 EXT. ASH BURIAL SIGHT. NEVADA DESERT. DAY. 49

HARRY and **NANCY** trundle along in a topless pick-up truck, the top has been broken off. **NANCY** looks very downcast.

HARRY isn't letting her out of his sight. They arrive at a massive pit in between two gigantic red rock formations, where a purposely covered in dust tarpaulin is attached to the ground by many pegs, but some of the pegs have come loose, and clouds of ash billow away with every gust. The pegs are old and have worn away. **HARRY** steps out of the vehicle, and walks towards the pit.

HARRY looks in quiet disgust at this failure. A man whimpers and emits incoherent apologies. **HARRY** keeps looking at the flapping tarpaulin.

50 INT. DOCTOR ENNIS OPPPENHEIMER'S SURGERY. DAY. 50

LUTHER sits in a sparse and dusty waiting room. There is a fan in the wall. The fan is opposite **LUTHER**, he slowly starts to go rather white in the face, and looks cold, bulbous and emaciated. He looks very ill. **LUTHER** looks around in a bit of a panic, he stands up and walks outside again.

51 EXT. OUTSIDE OPPENHEIMER'S SURGERY. DAY. 51

The scorching sun, within moments turns his face to how it was. He breathes a sigh of relief. He looks down to the ground, worried.

From outside we see **DR.OPPENHEIMER** step out of his door to call **LUTHER** in from outside. **LUTHER** walks back in.

52 INT. DR. OPPENHEIMER'S SURGERY. DAY. 52

DR. OPPENHEIMER is about 5 foot 10, and has a two-day beard, and is about fifty four. He has a hip-flask in his hand, which he drinks from.

OPPENHEIMER

Mr. Teller?

52 CONTINUED: 52

LUTHER
Oh, sorry.

OPPENHEIMER
I thought you'd got bored of waiting and left.

LUTHER
Oh no!

OPPENHEIMER
Well it happens a lot here.

LUTHER
That's, very strange.

OPPENHEIMER
Not to me it ain't... anyway come on in. You aren't from around here?

LUTHER
I'm from out of town.

OPPENHEIMER
You can say that again.

The two of them walk from the waiting room through to **OPPENHEIMER'S** surgery room.

OPPENHEIMER
Take a seat Mr. Teller... Now what are you here for?

LUTHER does not know where to begin.

LUTHER
Well, uh, I'm not really sure where to start... um, do you have any records going back the last 20-30 years?

OPPENHEIMER
At one point yeah, but they disappeared a long time ago.

LUTHER
(Annoyed.)
What happened?

OPPENHEIMER
They just disappeared. One day they were there, and the next they weren't, about 18 years ago that happened now.
(MORE)

52 CONTINUED: (2) 52

OPPENHEIMER (CONT'D)
But y'know it places like these they just throw everything out and hardly anyone goes to the doctor anyway.

LUTHER
Did you know anyone called Teller? Here in the town from years ago?

OPPENHEIMER
I only came here five years ago, apparently, I'm not good enough for their piece of shit hospitals. But, it may be the case that they moved away when the Proving Grounds were set up y'know for the weapons testing.

LUTHER
Really? Did that happen?

OPPENHEIMER
Yeah, there was quite an exodus from these parts when that happened, these folks either left things behind which were bulldozed, destroyed and buried or took everything with them. Our records would have been scrapped before, if y'ask me, they took all the records with them.

LUTHER
(confused and thinking.)
Yeah, okay.

OPPENHEIMER
Any how, what's the matter with you?

LUTHER
I uh, I had cancer. I recovered from it though.

OPPENHEIMER looks far more interested now. Starts to take notes.

OPPENHEIMER
What type was it?

LUTHER
That's just the thing, know one knows.
(MORE)

(CONTINUED)

LUTHER (CONT'D)
They said it was an occult cancer, but even after analyzing tissue samples, they couldn't find what kind it was.

OPPENHEIMER
God, how strange.

OPPENHEIMER
How long did you have the cancer for before you recovered?

LUTHER
Two months. I was literally on deaths door, but then three days later I was better than ever.

OPPENHEIMER looks slightly mystified and a little nervous.

LUTHER
Why do you ask?

OPPENHEIMER
We had some cases similar to that here, just a few years ago.

LUTHER'S eyes swell at the possibility of being enlightened.

LUTHER
Do you know what the cause is?

OPPENHEIMER
No, it's like you said, there's nothing to see, and only like five people have survived it.

LUTHER
Who are these people?

OPPENHEIMER
I'm sorry but I'm not at liberty to-

LUTHER
(Angry.)
I think under the circumstances-

OPPENHEIMER
How did you know about me? How did you get my name?

LUTHER
I talked to an older lady today, who lives in a shack on the edge of town.

OPPENHEIMER
You mean Gerry Lee?

LUTHER
What? Yes I think that might have been her name, I think I saw it on some paperwork in his house.

OPPENHEIMER
She died this morning.

LUTHER
What?! No, I was just talking to her!

OPPENHEIMER
I identified her with dental records, he is most certainly a stiff!

LUTHER
(Looks away in shock.)
Jesus Christ...

OPPENHEIMER
Mr. Teller, could I ask what you were talking about with Ms. Lee?

LUTHER
Yeah, it was just what I've been asking you but also she said she had been finding piles of ash with bone in it.

OPPENHEIMER looks really mystified. He walks over to a drawer cabinet, he opens it, and all his equipment is seen, apart from a stethoscope, the slot in the drawer fabric is there but, the instrument is not.

OPPENHEIMER
What the fuck!?

LUTHER
What? WHAT IS IT?

OPPENHEIMER
My stethoscope is gone.

LUTHER
Maybe someone broke in?

52 CONTINUED: (5) 52

OPPENHEIMER
To steal a stethoscope?

LUTHER
Does another Doctor work here?

53 EXT. OUTSIDE DOCTOR OPPENHEIMER'S SURGERY. DAY. 53

A massive great man ducks underneath the window and holds the stethoscope to the window. He whispers into a walkie-talkie.

54 INT. OPPENHEIMERS SURGERY. DAY. 54

OPPENHEIMER
NO! And I have the only key. Ok ok, wait a minute... I'll have to just miss the first part of the test...fuck!

OPPENHEIMER pulls out a giger-counter from a drawer.

He holds the counter up to **LUTHER.**

The counter crackles and gurgles. As **OPPENHEIMER** moves the device about **LUTHER** the dial shoots off the meter and it pops and bangs and a puff of smoke comes out of it.

LUTHER
WHAT! WHAT THE HELL JUST HAPPENED? WHY DID IT DO THAT?

OPPENHEIMER
By the laws of medicine you should be long gone Mr. Teller, but you are most certainly fully irradiated.

LUTHER
But I've never been irradiated! I had a few scans of my body with my cancer, but that wouldn't do that. AND I WAS NO WHERE NEAR THE TEST ZONES!!!

OPPENHEIMER
Maybe that's why someone doesn't want you learnin' about your folks.

54 CONTINUED: 54

LUTHER
... Oh Fuck, you're right! B-but WHO!? AND WHY?! None of this makes any sense..., why would they care? Who were the others who recovered from this? Who were they...?

OPPENHEIMER
Umm...

LUTHER
I won't tell anyone, please! I need to know, even if it involves something I don't want to hear-

(Seeing Oppenheimer's expression).

LUTHER
-I have no interest in making trouble for anyone, please I just want and need to know...please.

OPPENHEIMER looks at **LUTHER** for a few moments, deciding.

OPPENHEIMER
Look it's a really tight assed town this Mr. Teller, it has all these fucking rules you know and... you didn't hear any of this from me, okay. I don't know all their names, but I do know there was this girl, and I'm not sure if she's still here or not, she came to see me with a similar complaint.

LUTHER pricks up at this, wondering. Taking it all in.

LUTHER
There is something else I have noticed doctor... I need heat...

OPPENHEIMER
(more intrigued.)
What?

LUTHER
I need heat, I can't function in any other temperature apart from baking heat! At night and with your air conditioner I could hardly breath.
(MORE)

54 CONTINUED: (2) 54

LUTHER (CONT'D)
At night I have to hold the light bulbs in my hands or my mouth while they are on, and have showers with no cold in order to keep feeling well. What's wrong with me.

OPPENHEIMER
Look, I-I think you need to go now, I think you need to leave town and go back home, forget this place and see a more experienced and specialist Doctor. My best advice to you is to leave. I don't think you're going to find anything here Mr. Teller, let alone what you are looking for.

OPPENHEIMER looking very worried.

LUTHER
Okay...

LUTHER gets up and sees himself out.

Just as **LUTHER** is opening the door **OPPENHEIMER** stops him.

OPPENHEIMER
Just a sec Mr. Teller, one thing I can tell you without violating Doctor-patient confidentiality is that this girl, I found this strange at the time. She had really dirty black skin around her hands and really dirty nails.

LUTHER
Like oil or grease?

OPPENHEIMER
Yeah, something like that.

LUTHER looks round in despair and worry.

LUTHER
Thanks Doctor, goodbye.

LUTHER leaves. **OPPENHEIMER** holds his hand in his face.

OPPENHEIMER
(To himself.)
What's going on? Fuck this!

54 CONTINUED: (3) 54

OPPENHEIMER goes into his lobby, and lifts the receiver on his phone. He dials. He is shaking.

OPPENHEIMER
(Stammering.)
H-hello, c-c-could I please get the Sheriff's department.

55 INT. LUTHER'S MOTEL ROOM. DAY. 55

LUTHER is rapidly packing his bags.

56 EXT. NEVADA DESERT. DUSK. 56

Camera watches as **LUTHER'S** truck races down the track with a massive dust trail in pursuit.

Camera sees Luther's speed dial creep towards full speed.

Gravel ricochets off Luther's hub caps.

As he speeds down the track, he gets a fright, he sees a nuclear bomb cloud in front of him for a split second.

Then **LUTHER'S** truck explodes in a cloud of fire.

Camera watches the heap of metal just burn for some moments. Is **LUTHER** dead?

The door of the car gets slammed several times. Then it opens. A flaming **LUTHER** spills out onto the track. He screams in pain. He crawls on all fours leaving little burning fragments of clothing behind. He crawls aimlessly forward on all fours.

Close on: a shot that slowly tracks back watching **LUTHER'S** agonized face as he crawls. **LUTHER** slumps down to his stomach...dead?

Camera watches the car and **LUTHER** burn and slowly fades out.

FADE OUT TO:

57 EXT. NEVADA DESERT. DUSK. 57

The car is only smoking a bit.

LUTHER is naked on the road. He lies face-down. His hair and skin are not burned and are in-tact apart from a few small burns. He wakes up. He slowly pulls himself away from his crispy clothes underneath him that have burned to him.

He pauses. He closes his eyes and looks up into the sky. In desperation and shock horror at what is happening to him. He starts to shuffle back towards to towns ship.

DISSOLVE TO:

58 EXT. DESERT. EVENING. 58

LUTHER with his hands crossed over his groin shuffles along the track breathing quickly. He grunts as he treads on little rocks and sharp shrubs.

59 EXT. OUTSIDE HARRY'S HOUSE. NIGHT. 59

LUTHER gets back to **HARRY'S** place. He shuffles discreetly round the outside and looks carefully into windows. He peers into a sitting room, with papers and eaten legs of chicken meat. He moves along to a room with girls clothes and underwear in it, presumably **NANCY'S. LUTHER** crouches down next to this window waiting for **NANCY.**

A large rumble of thunder is heard. **LUTHER** flinches, and looks behind him, to see a very brooding, dark sky. He sees **NANCY** come out of the metal chamber next to Harry's garage with towels round her shoulders.

LUTHER peers in again subtly to check. He sees **HARRY** inside in the hall outside **NANCY'S** room. **HARRY** ties his boot lace meticulously, then stands up and walks away. **NANCY** walks into the room, her skin is flushed, yet rich and golden looking. She turns and shuts the door. She sits on the bed and takes her shoes off.

LUTHER taps on her window. **NANCY** gets a fright and goes to the window.

59 CONTINUED: 59

NANCY
YOU'RE NAKED! What are you doin'?
What's happened?

LUTHER
SSSHH!!! My car was... I-

NANCY
What Luther?

LUTHER
My car exploded.

NANCY throws **LUTHER** a towel, he ties it round his waist. **NANCY** uses all her strength to help **LUTHER** pull himself up into the room.

NANCY
OH MY GOD!! ARE YOU ALRIGHT???
Are you alright Luther, you're burned! Where were ya' goin'?

LUTHER realizes he is going to have to lie.

LUTHER
I was gonna... I was gonna drive to the next valley for a bit to see if they knew anythin' about my folks. Yes, I'm alright, I think I got out in time, but my clothes got burned. I didn't know where to go. Do you have anything I can wear?

NANCY
Uh, yes of course! Hang on.

She runs out of the room. **LUTHER** sits on the bed, he sits out of view of the door. **NANCY** comes back with some of **HARRY'S** clothes.

NANCY
Here, it ain't much but it should do!

LUTHER
Thanks so much.

NANCY averts her eyes as he puts the clothes on. She nervously chews a nail as she thinks, she is worried and concealing something.

59 CONTINUED: (2) 59

LUTHER
(Quietly.)
What were you all doin' in that metal chamber?

NANCY
(On the spot.)
Oh...uh... we have town meetings in there.

NANCY'S face sinks when she realizes what a useless excuse that was to say.

LUTHER
How come the rest of the towns people don't attend?

NANCY
(Avoids Luther's eye.)
Uh, well it's really a family meeting really, with Uncle Harry, and the people who work for him, it's just to... uh... get briefed on what the next project is that needs to be taken care of.

LUTHER agrees, but senses something strange.

LUTHER, looks in confusion to himself, and then slowly looks at **NANCY**, who is still not looking at him.

NANCY
Look, Luther, you can't stay here. Uncle Harry would kill us both if he caught us... sex after marriage and all.

LUTHER
No, sure!

NANCY
Go to Tritium's bar and wait for me there... Here's some money.

NANCY gives him 15 dollars out of her pocket.

NANCY
That should keep you goin' until I get there.

59 CONTINUED: (3) 59

LUTHER
Thanks very much Nancy... you've been very kind to me.

NANCY smiles nervously.

NANCY
Now go!

She beckons him out of the window in her room. **LUTHER** grabs and squeezes her hand for a second before he goes. They look at each other for a few moments. **NANCY** stays and watches him run away for a short while. She looks very sad. She gets up, closes the window and turns round. She flinches violently as she gets a massive fright. **HARRY** is standing in her room looking at her blankly. **NANCY** gazes nervously up at him.

60 EXT. TOWNSHIP STREET. EVENING. 60

HARRY walks along the sidewalk. He walks with purpose, he is headed somewhere. He spots **RAFE. RAFE** is staring at him as he does. **HARRY** turns round stares back at him with chilling focus. **RAFE** starts to get all upset. He starts to cry. **HARRY** draws closer. **RAFE** falls to the ground in terror. **HARRY** stands over him looking at him while **RAFE** shakes and screams in terror on the ground.

Shot is seen from **RAFES'S** POV, we see through his eyes as if the camera was behind his pupils looking through. So we see his moving pupils and iris like a ghost, opaque so we can see through them.

After doing this for a few beats more **HARRY** continues walking.

61 EXT. DESERT ROAD. OUTSIDE TOWN-SHIP. EVENING. 61

OPPENHEIMER speeds along a desert track away from the township. His car is clumbsily packed to suggest in was packed quickly.

Little inside mirror hangings chime and shake around with the movement of the car. Sweat runs down **OPPENHEIMER'S** face. He murmurs under his breath. His speed dials soar to top speed.

61 CONTINUED: 61

From in front, **OPPENHEIMER'S** car squeals on its breaks.

Camera pulls back a little to see the shadow of the massive truck with reinforced bull bars.

OPPENHEIMER looks in shock. He whimpers a little in panic. He looks behind him.

There is another massive pick-up truck with lights on full glare behind him which drives up from the desert onto the road.

OPPENHEIMER puts his hands on the steering wheel thinking. The track is quite wide and he sees a way around the truck in front of him. He looks behind. The second truck behind him is still there.

OPPENHEIMER looks ahead, he knows that it's the only escape. He stamps on the accelerator. The trucks make their moves too.

The two vehicles get closer and closer. **OPPENHEIMER** screams in terror not knowing what to do.

A filthy window with only **GRABLE'S** silhouette barrels towards him. **GRABLE** bellows in frenzied glee.

Close on: the grill of the truck, with the cab towering above it. The sound of the engine roaring.

OPPENHEIMER swerves round his aggressors and goes bumping off into the desert. The car is going so fast and can't take the terrain underneath, the axel breaks and some tires burst. **OPPENHEIMER** gets out and runs for his life.

He runs through the imposing pitch black desert, seeing far off lights disappear and reappear and hearing distant whoops. He whimpers and tries to grope his way through the blackness. He whimpers again, defeated when he sees and hears his car on fire in the distance. All goes very quiet apart from the distant burning car. He stays very still and listens.

The truck roars out of nowhere and **OPPENHEIMER** leaps out of the way. **DOMINIC SUNSET** leans out from inside the truck holding a long rope. He lassoes **OPPENHEIMER'S** neck.

61 CONTINUED: (2) 61

DOMINIC SUNSET, who is far too strong for the doctor holds the rope.

The trucks wheels spin but the truck doesn't move. **DOMINIC SUNSET** steps out of the truck and puts his end of the rope into the spinning tires of the truck which pulls **OPPENHEIMER** back with crushing speed and strength. **OPPENHEIMER** chokes and grabs the rope at his neck. **OPPENHEIMER** is pulled under the trucks wheel and is crushed

GRABLE bellows in excitement as this happens.

The aggressors drive off in a certain direction pulling the flaming wreckage of Oppenheimer's car into the desert.

FADE OUT:

62 EXT. NUCLEAR BOMB SITE. NIGHT. 62

A site in the desert concealed by its surrounding tall rocks. The two vehicles that were chasing **OPPENHEIMER** stop in front of a large metal cylinder with some of the men working on it. **HARRY** sits on a rock watching two men insert a large tube into it. **HARRY** sits by the light of a fire and lanterns, shaded and shadowed by the light, his face more blank than ever.

GRABLE exits the truck and goes to join his friend. **GRABLE** stands next to **HARRY.**

GRABLE
What else do we need?

HARRY
The cork is in the gun.

GRABLE
Good. How many times do you think he'll have to go back.

HARRY
This one is different, he knows what we need for this, and he knows where to get it. This one isn't guessing and hoping like the others. I think we'll only need one or two more, but I think just one more.

62 CONTINUED: 62

GRABLE nods.

HARRY looks into the horizon intensely. They look to the cylinder and then back to the horizon. They well up with emotion.

GRABLE
Harry, you know the chamber ain't workin' so good any more. Are you sure this is what'll do it?

HARRY nods silently.

HARRY and **GRABLE** are seen from behind with the fire and lantern light filtering between them.

FADE OUT:

63 EXT. DESERT ROAD. NIGHT. 63

Camera starts in an Ariel shot of the desert. The sound of a motor bike engine starts quietly and then quickly rises into a loud deafening roar.

WESTON barrels towards the town on his motor-bike, wearing a leather jacket twitching violently. He has a leather bag with him as well. His face twisted with worry.

64 INT. TRITIUM'S BAR. TOWNSHIP. NIGHT. 64

LUTHER sits at the counter with a drink, thinking, the bar is very smoky. **LUTHER** thinks, deep in thought.

Camera does a tracking shot around the front of **LUTHER** from behind the counter. It draws closer and closer to him whilst seeing a broad range of what is behind him, camera all the while is moving closer towards his face.

He remembers the explosion. In an agonising flash.

LUTHER
(Under his breath.)
What am I?

64 CONTINUED: 64

He takes another deep mouthful of his drink. He swirls the ice around in his glass. He ponders and looks into his glass.

A shot is seen of **LUTHER** through his drink as he finishes off the last dregs. Camera comes out of this and sees his face properly again. Camera tracks back, we see there are no locals behind **LUTHER** now. They have left the bar silently and **LUTHER** has not yet noticed.

LUTHER
(Looking up.)
Excuse me, I-...

LUTHER looks across the bar looking for a bartender. He turns, he now notices that no one else is in the bar. He looks, swerving around in worried confusion.

He turns back to his drink and considers this.

LUTHER hears the sound of the door open and then a rattle of **HARRY'S** snake rattle. We see blue overall wearing men come in behind **LUTHER** and stand behind him. **LUTHER** still facing towards the bar is listening and is becoming aware of people behind him.

LUTHER slowly looks round, his face twitches in horror when he sees who it is.

HARRY, GRABLE, BRAVO, IVY-MIKE and **DOMINIC SUNSET** stand behind **LUTHER** in the bar.

Camera pulls and tracks slowly back from **LUTHER.** Camera lifts up and over **HARRY** and his men revealing what is on the back of their overalls. Their names **GRABLE** and **CASTLE BRAVO** etc are written on the backs of their overalls with a mushroom cloud shaped pattern on the back of their overalls. On **HARRY'S** it says "Manhattan". **LUTHER** quivers. **DOMINIC SUNSET** still has a blood stained gas mask and a bloodied bandaged shoulder from where Gerry Lee shot him.

HARRY
Nancy isn't right about anything.

LUTHER grimaces and shakes his head in disbelief.

LUTHER
W-what... why are you here?

(CONTINUED)

64 CONTINUED: (2) 64

LUTHER gets off his bar stool now.

LUTHER
L-l-l-l-look, please, can't we talk about this? Think of Nancy...

Watching them walk forward towards him.

LUTHER
What sort of fucking uncle are you? Look, please don't, let me go, I'll...

LUTHER'S words dissolve into nothing, as he is so lost, he tries to go out the back way, but the two muscle men who have been staring at him in the town stand in his way. **LUTHER** stops and turns round to face **HARRY. HARRY** gives a nod to **DOMINIC SUNSET** who towers over **LUTHER** and blunders up to him, grabs his neck and pins him up against a wall with one arm. **LUTHER** choking, and drooling and getting purple in the face looks at **HARRY** as he approaches.

HARRY
(With quiet poison.)
You're going to give us what we need.

LUTHER cannot say anything as he is too choked.

Close on: **LUTHER'S** eye, the color in his Iris changes, it goes across a spectrum of color.

LUTHER turns his eyes to see a large ice bucket on the side of the bar with a bottle of beer in it.

With every morsel of strength he has left he puts his arms out to grab the bucket, his nails scraping its side. With his other hand he sinks his thumb into **DOMINIC SUNSET'S** gunshot wound. **DOMINIC SUNSET** bellows in pain at this. And this makes **DOMINIC SUNSET** relax his grip a bit which allows **LUTHER** to make the last stretch and reach the bucket.

HARRY sees this.

HARRY
WATCH OUT, HE'S-

LUTHER'S hand makes it into the bucket and vehemently grabs a beer bottle. He swings round and bottles **DOMINIC SUNSET** in the head.

DOMINIC SUNSET drops **LUTHER.** This attack knocks the mask off **DOMINIC SUNSET.** We see that **DOMINIC SUNSET** has no mouth or nose, only a tube, going into his throat, where the other end sticks out his pocket. Some of the skin on his face has stuck to the mask and tears away in strings from the mask. Cold beer splashes onto **DOMINIC SUNSET'S** face, this burns, melts and corrodes his skin as if it were acid.

LUTHER looks in realization, he realizes now why he feels ill in the cold and why **NANCY** can't leave and what hurts these people.

The ice cubes scattered on the floor have pieces of skin latched onto them.

HARRY and the group are shocked at their huge member being taken down, and his inhuman and relentless screaming.

DOMINIC SUNSET dares not touch his face because it is still cold and it would hurt his hands.

DOMINIC SUNSET screams so violently that his face at the part his mouth would have been splits, tearing his face open allowing an even more distressing scream out. His face disintegrating with the cold liquid on it. His tongue like a writhing anorexic tentacle.

LUTHER pours the ice from the ice bucket on **DOMINIC SUNSET'S** head, the cold weakens his skull allowing his head to crumble away.

LUTHER runs and reaches over the bar counter to their master ice bucket and throws ice cubes from it at **HARRY** and his group.

The group leap out of the path as if acid were being thrown at them. Some land awkwardly on their necks etc, hurting themselves. **HARRY** dodges but keeps his eyes fixed on **LUTHER.**

65 EXT. TOWNSHIP. EVENING. 65

LUTHER runs down the alley. Camera sees his feet from behind, dust flying into the face of the camera.

He looks at his hands, they are red, blistered and sore from the ice, he realizes he is beginning to suffer from the cold like the rest of them. He looks around for help.

66 EXT. OUTSIDE BAR. EVENING. 66

HARRY, angry, is pulling his men up from the ground.

HARRY
GET UP! I SAID GET UP!

The men look very worried and ashamed. They run out the door.

CUT BACK TO:

67 EXT. ALLEY. EVENING. 67

LUTHER is trying to scramble up a wall at the end of the alley. **HARRY** and his men run past the alley and then double take and come back and advance towards **LUTHER. LUTHER**, terrified backs up against the wall. **HARRY** drives a truck down into the alley arriving in the part of the alley that **LUTHER** is at, after the rest of his men.

HARRY exits the truck and goes up to **LUTHER**, everyone is silent. **HARRY** and his men stare at **LUTHER** and **LUTHER** stares only at **HARRY. HARRY** gestures to the truck.

HARRY
(Softly.)
Get in the truck.

LUTHER looks around not knowing what to do or say. **HARRY** points to the truck again.

HARRY
Get in the truck, go on get in.

LUTHER sees he is surrounded and doesn't have any choice in the matter.

(CONTINUED)

67 CONTINUED: 67

He gingerly goes round and gets in the truck. **HARRY** follows and gets into the driver's seat. Takes out the keys and starts the truck, the two set off.

68 INT. HARRY'S TRUCK. NIGHT. 68

A terrified **LUTHER** stares ahead out of the window into the darkness. He sneaks tiny glances at **HARRY** who looks ahead. **HARRY** then looks at him, **LUTHER** nervously meets his gaze. **LUTHER** is petrified at the gaze that is on him.

LUTHER
(Nervously and
quietly.)
Where are you taking me?

HARRY says nothing, he only looks at **LUTHER** with a very strange, tiny and vague almost sort of smirk on his face.

Through the truck windows we see the garage and the heat chamber appear out of the darkness, dimly lit.

69 EXT. HARRY'S FORE COURT. NIGHT. 69

The truck pulls up next to the strange metal structure that Nancy said was the town mortuary. The two men get out. **HARRY** walks round the other side of the truck to **LUTHER. LUTHER** is so terrified he bellows at and towards the kiosk building.

LUTHER
NANCY!!!!!!!

HARRY punches **LUTHER** so hard in the head he is knocked out. This takes us to black.

70 INT. HEAT CHAMBER. NIGHT. 70

A very soft and blurred shot is seen. With orangy, brownish, reddish colors. It starts to sharpen slightly until only **LUTHER** is in focus.

Camera sees the place as **LUTHER** does. It is very blurred through **LUTHER'S** eyes.

(CONTINUED)

70 CONTINUED: 70

LUTHER writhes around a bit trying to feel where he is. He rubs his eyes. He hears a clanking, he looks up. He snaps out of his fuzzy state.

The rest of his surroundings come into crisp focus too.

He jumps back with shock. He reels back against the wall.

He notices that his hand is cuffed to a pipe running along this chamber. He looks in horror at his new prison, he sees his arm is chained to a pipe. He has difficulty breathing in the heat. Twenty nozzles emit flame opposite him, they are low at the moment but grow in intensity and aural volume as this happens.

The wall **LUTHER** has his back to is like a very finely woven cage. A group of human figures are seen about three meters behind the mesh. They cannot be made out.

LUTHER
H- help... HELP!!! Please help me... get me out of here, please!

The figures turn idly to look at him, then assemble into a line and spread their arms slightly.

LUTHER realizes they aren't going to help him. He starts to writhe and squirm and tug at his chain to no avail. His hand just goes red and puffy.

LUTHER
(He tries pulling again.)
AAAAAAAAAHHHHHHHHHH!!!!!!!!!!!!!!

His clothes begin to smoke, grimacing he looks around for anything to help him. He sees an empty beer bottle lodged in the pipes. He strains to reach it but does just. **LUTHER** smashes the bottle, to create shards. He picks up the sharpest shard.

LUTHER hurriedly takes off one of his shoes, takes out the shoelace and ties it tightly around the wrist of his trapped arm. Next, he puts his shoe between his teeth. He starts to slice way the webbed flap of skin connecting his thumb and index finger. After this he pulls back his thumb to dislocate the joint and tear it away from his hand. He manages to do this with an amazing exertion of strength brought on by his pure panic.

70 CONTINUED: (2) 70

A strip of skin like cellotape still connects his detached thumb to his forearm, his efforts at severing it only tear a further strip up his forearm like cellotape. He is forced to cut it free with his glass shard. He gets free because he can pass his thumbless hand through the handcuff. He lurches towards the door and claws at it, but it is locked, he passes out with the heat.

DISSOLVE TO:

71 EXT. NEVADA DESERT. DAY. 71

A shot of the open desert is seen. A small dark figure on a motor bike draws closer and closer to the camera. It's **WESTON.**

WESTON is now seen careering along at top speed along the desert track leading into the town. He still looks distraught, the motor bike sound thunders out.

72 EXT. OUTSIDE HEAT CHAMBER. DAY. 72

The door to the chamber opens, and an unseen figure hauls **LUTHER** out and slams the door shut.

FADE UP TO:

73 EXT. NEVADA DESERT. DAWN. 73

A small crater in the surface of the desert. Surrounded by giant red rock formations. **LUTHER** lies almost naked on a blanket and has a thin cotton sheet over him. His burns are bandaged and he has a hot-water bottle over his head. **NANCY** sits beside him, still in her waitress uniform. **NANCY** looks at him, saddened. She then strokes the hair off his forehead.

LUTHER wakes with a start.

LUTHER
W-What? WHAT!!!!

LUTHER sees **NANCY.** He is angry and disgusted. He violently shakes off the blanket and stands up, having a fit and shaking with anger and disbelief.

(CONTINUED)

73 CONTINUED: 73

LUTHER
WHAT!? WHAT ARE YOU? WHAT ARE YOU PEOPLE?!

NANCY
(Begins to weep.)
Please Luther-

LUTHER
PLEASE NOTHING! I WAS NEARLY FUCKING KILLED!

NANCY
LUTHER,

LUTHER
WHAT!!!

NANCY
We're mutated.

LUTHER
THAT'S A...-

(babbles for words).

LUTHER
-CUNTING UNDERSTATEMENT!!!!!!

NANCY
Look Luther, there's something wrong with us and we don't know why, well at least, we don't know absolutely why, I mean they say that the bombs they're testin' are dirty and do terrible things to people. But these bombs they just kill ya' and the side affects do to, but we're still alive so we dunno really what is wrong with us.

LUTHER looks on worried and furious but knows he has to hear this. **NANCY** looks at him pleading that he understands.

LUTHER
I was gonna leave and you tried to kill me!

NANCY
Not me Luther.

LUTHER
It doesn't matter who, you, your so called uncle Harry or any of these goons.

LUTHER starts to walk into the desert towards the track leading into the town. **NANCY** jogs up to him.

NANCY
Luther... you have it too!

LUTHER
What?

NANCY
You have what we have, the mutation or whateva you want to call it.

LUTHER
How else do you think you survived that car crash? Or lasted so long in that heat chamber? And that's why we can't live without it, we need heat. It seems you are not fully there yet, it seems to take some months to settle in that's why you still burn and ice and cold don't really bother you yet.

LUTHER is appalled.

LUTHER
If you know more Nancy you've gotta tell me!

NANCY
It doesn't matter Luther we've got it and that's all -

LUTHER
TELL ME!!!!!!!

NANCY cries. **LUTHER** marches up to her and grabs her and shakes her.

LUTHER
TELL ME!!!

NANCY
(In sobs.)
We don't know for sure, we really don't, how people get this, but...

LUTHER
What does your uncle say? What's his theory, I'm real interested to hear that.

NANCY
Uncle Harry thinks that it's generational. If your ma or pa gets a full dose and then conceive then their children can then get it. I reckon ma folks got a right old dose when the testing began and then had me. Harry also says that some people's bodies respond differently, he talks about a sweet spot.

LUTHER
What the fuck is that?

NANCY
Where if you get it just right, like if you're just the right distance away from it.

LUTHER
From what?

NANCY
The explosions of the bombs.

LUTHER sort of laughs and cries and turns his head.

NANCY
But Luther it's ok, Uncle Harry is putting it right, he's found a way to put it right. If you can copy the sweet spot it will cure you. It stands to reason Luther.

LUTHER scoffs again. Realizes something more sinister.

LUTHER
So wait if this is true then Harry or whoever it is doesn't know I have it?

NANCY
Yes. That's why I suggested they blew your car up.

LUTHER is appalled.

LUTHER
You tried to kill me?

NANCY
NO! I knew you were turning from what you told me in the car, you remember Luther? It was you or us Luther and Uncle Harry felt you could find out and stop us getting the cure. I said for him to blow you up because I knew you'd survive and that you would leave.

LUTHER
If I'm one of you how am I supposed to leave?

NANCY
I don't know Luther, I just knew I had to do anything I could. You can't blame Harry Luther he was just trying to save us, and he was just getting rid of anything that could stop us all from being cured.

LUTHER
Wait a minute, replicate the sweet spot? What does that mean?

NANCY
Not all the tests work Luther. They tried an air test three years ago and they lost it and it didn't go off. Harry found it. He's figured it all out, he just needs a few more parts and he-

LUTHER
Nancy are you talking about the detonation of an atom bomb?

NANCY
It's the only way to get the sweet spot back again-

LUTHER
WHAT!!!!

NANCY
The other test sites are so heavily guarded we can't get near enough. We need to get 5 miles from ground zero-

LUTHER reels back in horror and shock, his reaction is immense to this.

LUTHER
NANCY THIS IS FUCKING CUNTING MADNESS!!!! THIS COULD KILL MILLIONS OF PEOPLE THIS IS THE MOST DANGEROUS THING YOU COULD DO IN THIS WORLD!!!! HOW DOES HE THINK THAT???

NANCY
We have to Luther, why should we always die so other people can live, we didn't ask for any of this to happen to us. We can cure you too Luther. It stands to reason anyway Luther. And you'll need one of these, I brought one for you.

A tear rolls down **LUTHER'S** face.

LUTHER
Stands to what??!! Don't change the subject.

NANCY
I'm not, you will need one of these, we can't survive below 20 degrees celsius. Anything below and we die. It starts to hurt at 26 and below.

NANCY hands **LUTHER** a small thermometer. **LUTHER** looks at it. It reads 28 degrees celsius at the moment.

NANCY
Luther there is one last thing I need to show you.

74 EXT. NEVADA DESERT. OUTSIDE HARRY'S HOUSE. NIGHT. 74

WESTON trundles up to Harry's garage/house. He turns up onto the fore-court concrete and slowly up to the door.

The door opens. **HARRY** stands in the door-frame, chomping on a leg of meat. **WESTON** looks up in fright. **WESTON'S** face twitches violently, he puts his hand over his face to try and calm it. **HARRY** cruelly copies, but without smiling or laughing at the cruelty.

74 CONTINUED: 74

HARRY

Got it?

WESTON

Yes.

HARRY closes the door behind them.

75 INT. HARRY'S GARAGE. MAIN ROOM DAY. 75

WESTON enters fearfully. **HARRY'S** main crew are also here. **HARRY** reaches his hand out to **WESTON** wanting **WESTON** to hand him the fruits of his mission.

WESTON does so. **HARRY** zealously takes them off him. **HARRY** flips through a folder of charts and diagrams.

WESTON stands there not knowing what to do with himself or where to position himself.

He looks around in slow jerks, trying not to draw too much attention to himself. He purses and clenches his face to try and stop the twitches.

HARRY looks at **WESTON** then back at **GRABLE. HARRY** nods to **GRABLE.**

The men apart from **HARRY** light up and smile and hug each other.

HARRY looks again to **GRABLE** his expression changes slightly here, as **GRABLE** is about the only person **HARRY** has any sort of connection with.

WESTON

(Whistles and beeps.)

Well if you're finished and, you... well... have everything... You can release my friend, and he and I can... be on our way. We won't tell anyone... please we just want to go home, I can't be bothered telling any one I really can't I just want rest. I've held up my end of the bargain.

HARRY and **GRABLE** exchange a glance.

75 CONTINUED: 75

WESTON
P-p-p-p-please! I swear to God we won't tell anyone-.

WESTON'S words die off.

WESTON sort of smiles to himself in realization at what has happened, he kind of knew it. He shakes his head at them with a new sort of bravery. **WESTON** seizes his chance, he runs and launches himself through a window. **HARRY'S** men run after him.

76 EXT. OUTSIDE HARRY'S HOUSE. NIGHT. 76

WESTON runs for his bike, sees he hasn't time he continues on foot. **GRABLE** is the fastest and really goes after **WESTON** they disappear into the dark desert.

77 EXT. DESERT BEHIND HARRY'S HOUSE. NIGHT. 77

NANCY and **LUTHER** walk up behind the metal chamber about 20 yards from **HARRY'S** garage, having just missed all that happened at the garage. Camera shows **WESTON** and **GRABLE** run across the fore court into the desert. But **NANCY** and **LUTHER** are approaching the heat chamber which blocks them from seeing **GRABLE** and **WESTON** running away.

78 EXT. OUTSIDE HEAT CHAMBER. NIGHT. 78

NANCY leads **LUTHER** up to the chamber where the door is. She looks at him before she starts to take her clothes off.

LUTHER
(Shocked.)
What the hell are we doing here?

NANCY
You just need to start slowly and build up and you'll be fine.

LUTHER
But-

NANCY
-Trust me Luther, trust me.

(CONTINUED)

78 CONTINUED: 78

LUTHER relents a bit to her will, he has trusted her this far.

NANCY
You need to do it too Luther, don't worry we're all human it's nothing we haven't seen before.

LUTHER hesitantly and shakily starts to take his clothes off. **LUTHER** goes down to his underwear and stops. **NANCY** goes all the way to full nakedness.

NANCY
Them too Luther, they'll burn just like the other things.

LUTHER takes them off. They both find something incredibly sensual and sexual about this. They breath heavily and jerkily. **NANCY** looks at him one more time before leading him in.

We see a shot of these two naked bodies from the rear hold hands and walk into the chamber. There is a reddish light in the chamber illuminating them from in front.

79 INT. HEAT CHAMBER. NIGHT. 79

On entrance we see the blackened metal space from earlier. There are two tiers to the chamber. One is a small standing space, and separating this from the second larger tier is a dense metal mesh.

LUTHER
(Nervously.)
What's the metal fence for?

NANCY
Ash blowing hard at you hurts...ssh.

NANCY turns some taps on the wall next to the two of them. The nozzles at the other end begin to hiss. Next she pushes a button on the wall. A small spark occurs at the other end igniting the gas. The flow starts slowly and **NANCY** builds it up slowly by turning the taps to open them up more. She takes terrified **LUTHER'S** hand and smiles at him, she spreads her arms and closes her eyes, **LUTHER** copies. The flame builds up and is now blasting full furnace flame at them. They quietly gasp.

79 CONTINUED: 79

We see a few shots of the swimming fire rippling over through the mesh to **LUTHER** and **NANCY.**

DISSOLVE TO:

80 INT. HEAT CHAMBER. NIGHT. 80

The fire is out and **LUTHER** and **NANCY** are getting dressed again. They are incredibly flushed. **NANCY** walks round the side of the chamber and comes back with a tire iron. She hands it to **LUTHER.**

NANCY
Bend it. Just do it.

LUTHER hesitantly tries and succeeds to bend the iron, his face, displays great shock and astonishment at his achievement.

NANCY
You'll have to do this at least once a week and this-

NANCY points to the bent tire iron. **LUTHER** has a sort of hypnotized expression on his face.

NANCY
-this will last about eight hours after every dose. Now stay here Luther, I'll go in and straighten things out with Uncle Harry.

LUTHER
(Protests in shock.)
But, what if-

NANCY
I know my Uncle, Luther, I'll be fine, you just stay here and please don't come in, no matter what you hear don't come in, trust me Luther I'll be fine.

LUTHER sees he must trust her and can see that his presence would only inflame the situation and could endanger **NANCY** more than his absence. **LUTHER** nods. **NANCY** runs round to go in to see **HARRY.**

81 EXT. DESERT. NIGHT. 81

WESTON runs through the desert at full pelt. **GRABLE** follows in hot pursuit. Thunder and lightning start to crash and boom in the sky. This continues over this whole sequence. **WESTON** looks round and sees **GRABLE** gaining on him.

Panorama of them is seen of them running in the distance, **GRABLE** closing the gap between them. An enormous dust cloud enters frame, the two are heading straight for it. The dust and wind are very loud and drown out all other sound human and otherwise.

WESTON can only see a few feet in front of himself with the dust. He shields his eyes and looks for **GRABLE**. He gropes around trying to find his bearings.

GRABLE erupts out of the dust and pummels **WESTON** knocking **WESTON** to the ground. **WESTON** is struck by a stroke of great luck. A snake hissing and coiled is near **WESTON**. **WESTON** as fast as the snake itself picks up and throws the snake at **GRABLE** the snake latches onto **GRABLE'S** cheek bone. Screaming and cascading blood from **GRABLE** ensue from this.

WESTON sees his chance for the final blow, he grabs **GRABLE'S** cheek from inside his mouth, and pulls back, pushing back off **GRABLE'S** shoulder for grip, he pulls **GRABLE'S** cheek back, slowly tearing it off.

WESTON falls back bellowing and crying in effort, release, trauma and shock holding **GRABLE'S** cheek. He sees his chance and runs into the dust.

82 INT. HARRY'S KITCHEN. NIGHT. 82

The dust storm still rages outside the window. Deep rolls of thunder ring out through this sequence every now and then.

We open on a very grounded shot showing **NANCY** sitting at one end of their large kitchen table looking away. The back of **HARRY'S** head is seen looking in the other direction. They sit in silence.

82 CONTINUED: 82

HARRY looks over at **NANCY** who is still not looking at him. Something happens in **HARRY'S** face. He has changed the way he thinks of **NANCY,** for the worse. He turns and stares at her. Camera holds on **HARRY** staring for a few beats.

NANCY wears some very warm clothes because of her condition of course.

NANCY feels this and slowly looks round worried and frightened. Her face cowers further when she realizes she is being stared at. She very anxiously looks elsewhere.

HARRY'S face does not relent his intimidating stare.

When **NANCY** speaks here, she is simultaneously copied by **HARRY.**

NANCY	HARRY
Please Uncle Harry-	Please Uncle Harry-

NANCY flinches in fear and astonishment at this. She looks at the floor for a few moments, and then looks back at **HARRY.**

NANCY	HARRY
What are you doing that for?	What are you doing that for?
NANCY (Starts to sob.) Uncle please!	HARRY (Copies sobbing sounds.) Uncle please!
NANCY I just didn't want us to all die UNCLE BECAUSE OF (gets louder) A MISTAKE!!! YOU CAN'T KILL US!! PLEASE TRY TO UNDERSTAND AND PLEASE STOP THIS (grabs her hair) VIOLENCE UNCLE PLEASE, PLEASE.	HARRY I just didn't want us to all die UNCLE BECAUSE OF (gets louder too) A MISTAKE!!! YOU CAN'T KILL US!! PLEASE TRY TO UNDERSTAND AND PLEASE STOP THIS (grabs his hair) VIOLENCE UNCLE PLEASE, PLEASE.
NANCY (Screaming in sobbing tears.) AAAAHHHHH PLEASE STOP!!!! PLEASE!!!!!!	HARRY (Copies tears as well.) AAAAAAAHHHH!!!! PLEASE STOP!!!!!!! PLEASE!!!!!

NANCY purses her eyes, leans flat on the table and screams.

(CONTINUED)

82 CONTINUED: (2) 82

NANCY
AAAAAHHHHHHH!!!!!!!!!

HARRY
(Does same.)
AAAAAAAAHHHHHHH!!!!!!!!

NANCY runs out of energy. She sobs. **HARRY** stops the copying.

HARRY stands up and begins to slowly walk towards her. He stares at her. She cowers and cries. He gently slaps her with the back of his hand across her cheek. **NANCY** wraps her arms round her head crying. She crumples into her chair, to avoid being hit.

NANCY whimpers and cries, while **HARRY** semi-circles her never taking his severe and unrelenting gaze off her. He slaps the top of her head with the front of his hand. She whimpers and jerks away.

NANCY
Uncle! Please!

HARRY
Uncle! Please!

HARRY shoves her, so she nearly falls off her chair. He slaps her with the back of his hand again very hard.

The slaps and strikes become more frequent and harder. **HARRY** next, actually showing some anger picks her up by the hair and drags her along the ground.

NANCY shrieks and laments in pain and fear as she is dragged by her hair. She puts her hands up to try and soften the force on her hair.

-- IN LIVING ROOM -- **HARRY** arrives into the room, there is a rickety wooden table in the middle of the room.

HARRY picks screaming **NANCY** up from behind, raiser her above his head and smashes her into the table, the table disintegrating under the impact.

He picks a wounded and shaken **NANCY** up and tosses her with devastating strength and speed into a table with things on it, she collides into a table and the wall, objects go flying.

HARRY looks around the room thinking. He walks round to **NANCY** and throws her full pelt into the arm chair, the pillows do little to soften the blow.

82 CONTINUED: (3) 82

She collapses to the ground, bruised and bloodied. She rolls over, eyes barely open. **HARRY** lifts the faded sofa in the room up onto it's other arm. He pushes it violently and it careers over and lands on **NANCY** with crushing force.

83 EXT. BEHIND HEAT CHAMBER. NIGHT. 83

LUTHER obediently stays where **NANCY** told him to. Until he hears wails for help in the desert.

WESTON
(In distance in desert.)
HELP!!!!! HELP ME!!!!

The voice is relatively near. He looks round to **HARRY'S** garage, then back out to the screaming voice in the desert. He runs to go and see who is calling for help.

84 EXT. DESERT. NIGHT. 84

The yells for help are throughout this sequence. **LUTHER** shields his eyes and strains to see through the dust storm, even though it is now dying. He tries to follow the yells.

LUTHER
HELLO! ARE YOU ALRIGHT?

Out of nowhere **WESTON** dives up to **LUTHER** lands on his knees and grabs **LUTHER'S** shirt and starts to beg.

WESTON
Help me Luther! Help me!

WESTON starts to babble incoherently.

LUTHER
(In shock.)
L- what, I- Are you- Are you alright? Are you alright?

WESTON
He tried to kill me he was trying... to kill...me.

WESTON slumps into **LUTHER'S** grasp and faints. **LUTHER** exclaims at his predicament. He drags **WESTON** away.

85 INT. HARRY'S HOUSE. NIGHT. 85

HARRY goes into a sort of frenzy pummelling **NANCY** into the ground. We hold on this for a few more beats.

(We stay in the room with **NANCY**). **HARRY** exits the room and walks back with rope.

HARRY goes about tying **NANCY** up. A police siren is heard loudly from outside. **HARRY** looks round, his expression is back to normal now.

A high-way patrol car with its flashing lights waits in **HARRY'S** garage fore-court. Two officers get out the car. They match the bad cop and good cop look, the bad one chews tobacco, the good cop tries and fails to look brooding. The bad cop, older and gruff, the young cop, baby faced and naive.

The **BAD COP** points to a pump and the **YOUNG COP** fills their car.

BAD COP
Fill'er up!

The **YOUNG COP** goes about filling the car up.

HARRY walks out to see them, noticing they are taking his petrol, most likely with no intention of paying for it.

HARRY has wrapped a jacket round himself. The two officers walk up to see him.

HARRY
Is there a problem officers?

BAD COP
Well mister, we've received an unidentified call from somewhere in this area, saying that a group of thugs were intimidating residents in the area. Have you heard of such a thing?

HARRY
Can't say I have.

BAD COP
Look, I understand if they threatened you, but you need to tell us if you know something.

HARRY
It's a quiet place here, nothing of any sort happens round here... if someone completes a cross-word without any help that's news around here. Really officer it sounds like a prank call... I wouldn't be surprised if some kids got bored,.. As I said there isn't much going on around here. If you don't have any more questions officer I really would like to get back to my business, it's been a long day.

The **BAD COP** ignores this.

BAD COP
You look like one of these Nancy boys from Vegas... the shemale Jessie chicks with dicks, girls when dressed boys when naked variety. Now jerkweed, do I look like I have my thumb up my ass and a sign on my car saying two cunts in this car.

HARRY
Feel free to come in and have a look around.

BAD COP
That's what I thought I heard dickweed!

The **YOUNG COP** stays outside, he chews tobacco and scowls at **HARRY, HARRY** looks at him for a second in a cold and emotionless way. Then turns to follow the **BAD COP** in.

BAD COP
You live on the out-skirts of this town, you see all the comings and goings... are you sure you didn't see anything out of place?

HARRY
Like I said.

85 CONTINUED: (2) 85

The **BAD COP** walks into the kiosk building. Spitting inside the building.

The kiosk area is a bit messed up.

BAD COP
What sort'a fuckin' queer shit's bin' goin' on here faggot?

HARRY looks at the juice the **BAD COP** spat out when he says this, the **BAD COP** notices this.

HARRY
Not all my customers are as respectful of my property as I would hope, they tend to make a mess.

BAD COP
Would you stay here, I don't want you follwin' me, hidin' things you might not want me to see or find along the way, you got that faggot!? Whether it be a bloody fuckin' corpse or your butt plugs. Or your special fuckin' teenie twinkie friend.

The **BAD COP** takes out a large revolver, smiles mockingly at **HARRY** and continues his search.

86 EXT. HARRY'S GARAGE. NIGHT. 86

The **YOUNG COP** looks suspicious, wondering what's going on.

87 INT. HARRY'S HOUSE. NIGHT. 87

The **BAD COP** makes his way through the cramped and dark halls of **HARRY'S** house.

BAD COP
(To himself.)
What kinda' fuckin' shit hole is this place. What sorta' fuckin' gay bar are you runnin' here? Are ya' a fuckin' rent boy with bondage ir somethin'?

(CONTINUED)

87 CONTINUED: 87

The **BAD COP** makes his way to **HARRY'S** bath-room and then **HARRY'S** kitchen, he turns his face up at what he sees. He hears a grunt. He freezes and aims his weapon. He walks into **HARRY'S** living room.

The **BAD COP** sees the smashed up room with spots of blood everywhere. His eyes meet **NANCY'S** eyes. He looks in shock. He takes his walkie-talkie and starts to speak into it.

BAD COP

Send for-

At this, the cop turns round and comes face to face with **HARRY.** In a lightning flash **HARRY** with a large mechanics spanner bludgeons the **BAD COP'S** head and it explodes at this.

After this, **HARRY** remains standing in the door-frame with the large mechanic's spanner, it has hair and blood on it. He looks ahead blankly towards **NANCY.**

HARRY turns round again as he hears chatter out-side. He marches out-side.

88 EXT. OUTSIDE HARRY'S GARAGE. NIGHT. 88

The **YOUNG COP** presses and fiddles with his walkie-talkie, with only fuzz heard.

POLICE OFFICER

Sir! Sir... are you okay? Do I need to send for back up?

Camera follows **HARRY** as he steps down the steps onto his garage fore-court, still holding the spanner. He walks relentlessly up to the **YOUNG COP.** The **YOUNG COP** just notices. He fumbles for his gun.

Before he has his gun in his hands.

POLICE OFFICER

FREEZE!

HARRY does not freeze, instead he strikes the **YOUNG COP** across the face with his spanner, teeth and blood go flying.

88 CONTINUED: 88

HARRY drops the spanner, picks up the **YOUNG COP** with one arm and slams him onto the bonnet, next **HARRY** takes a petrol pump and pushes it through the **YOUNG COPS'** lips and teeth, jamming it down his throat pumping petrol in simultaneously, he fellates the petrol pump in and out of the **YOUNG COPS'** mouth through sickening gurgling and choking until the **YOUNG COP** is dead.

HARRY shuts off the petrol and puts the pump back. Leaving the dead **YOUNG COP** sprawled out on the bonnet of the car.

We see blood and petrol making its way across the shiny bonnet and then pouring off onto the dusty concrete.

HARRY then gets his act together, he goes about dealing with the body of the Young Cop.

JUMP CUT:

HARRY throws the cops into the back-seat of their car. He walks round the back of his building, and finds some rope. He comes back and sets about rigging the car to accelerate away without a driver by tying the accelerator down to the floor.

HARRY puts in and turns ignition key.

HARRY stumbles away from it as it moves, he slams the door shut and the car races away bumping along into the desert.

HARRY watches it disappear into the desert.

-- In Cop Car -- The bodies flail and bump around. The body in the back falls into the foot area.

The dust storm in now over.

89 EXT. DESERT. NIGHT. 89

LUTHER and **WESTON** sit in mounds of dust covered in dust themselves next to some rocks. **WESTON** stirs, **LUTHER** sees this.

LUTHER
H-Hello-

WESTON gets a huge jump and falls back, in a cloud of dust, he scrambles to his feet, fending off **LUTHER**.

WESTON
GET BACK AARRHHGGG!!!! GO AWAY!!!!! FUCK OFF!!! GET LOST!!!! AHHHHAAA!!!! I'LL KILL YOU!!!!!

LUTHER
(Making diplomatic hand gestures.)
NO NO NO!!!!! I'm not one of them! I'm not with them!

WESTON stops and is poised to run.

LUTHER
(Continuing hand motions.)
NO WAIT!! PLEASE!!! I'M ON YOUR SIDE!!!!

WESTON still in position looks round.

WESTON
Who are you? Who are these people? What do you want with me? Why did you come and find me?

LUTHER
It was a long shot I would find you, but I am so pleased I did, because what I need to do I can't do on my own.

WESTON
What are you talking about?

LUTHER
Can we, just - sit down on the ground and talk?

WESTON looks defensive again.

LUTHER
(Noticing.)
I mean, I'll sit here, and you can sit where you are, okay? We should just calm down.

89 CONTINUED: (2) 89

WESTON thinks for a few moments, he breathes heavily. He slowly sits down. **LUTHER** does like-wise.

WESTON
You better give me some answers!

LUTHER
I hope the same.

They nod, they understand each other and both calm down.

LUTHER
I'm Luther Teller, I came to this town to find answers, ironically to find out about my family who I think used to live here. They died from a weird form of cancer and I wanted to see if I could learn more about it.

WESTON nods.

LUTHER
Right, so I couldn't let it lie, I knew something had to have caused it, and I too had this cancer but I got better from it, from deaths door to fighting fit within 24 hours, I knew there had to be more to it.

WESTON
Why did you not just get out, why look for me?

LUTHER
I couldn't just stand by and watch them kill somebody else, knowing what I know.

WESTON
Well you were a bit late.

LUTHER
Yes, but it was the-

WESTON
Dust storm, I Know, it just would've been helpful...
(MORE)

89 CONTINUED: (3) 89

WESTON (CONT'D)
We were..., me and some friends were going to a funeral, and we got stopped at a roadblock, the cops there were in on it too, they sent us off into the middle of nowhere, then before we knew it we were tortured in this metal box-

LUTHER knows of what he is talking about.

LUTHER
- I've been in that box too.

WESTON looks up in amazement, **LUTHER** nods to him.

LUTHER holds up his bloody, clothed hand.

LUTHER
I had to tear my thumb off to get out... they turned whatever it was originally into a furnace.

WESTON
How come you're not burnt?

LUTHER
B... because it seems that, if you recover from this... cancer... this whatever it is, you can survive inhuman amounts of heat, and you need weekly doses of this extreme heat to stay alive. I learned this from a local girl.

WESTON
Wait a minute-

LUTHER
- My car was blown up with me in it... my clothes were all burnt off, but I was left with hardly a scratch, do you know what this means? I've never even heard of anything like it in my life.

WESTON shakes his head.

WESTON
What does it mean? Are you saying it's fall out or something?

(CONTINUED)

89 CONTINUED: (4) 89

LUTHER
Well... whose to say really, but it appears that way. It means I have to keep getting heat once every week, or I die... or I get cured if there is one... The thing is my friend, that local girl I am talking about has this Uncle or something she lives with and he's been killing people. And they seem to have this mad theory about how to cure this condition or whatever it is. They claim they have an atom bomb and think something about its detonation will cure them, it's fucking madness!!!

WESTON
Jesus Christ... are you serious?...I wasn't, they killed... they asked us all these weird questions about what our professions were and what we had academically studied... I mean what do you say to that?

LUTHER
What happened next?

WESTON
They destroyed everyone in the room apart from me and my friend Kurt. They took Kurt away... well the understanding was if I didn't do what they wanted Kurt died... but I think they killed him the moment they were out of the chamber... Th-

WESTON looks up in terror, realizing something.

WESTON
Oh, Jesus, oh my God!

LUTHER
(Worried and concerned.)
What? What is it?

WESTON
Oh my God... when they let me out the heat chamber, I mean, regarding the things they wanted me to do, they wanted me to bring back plans of detonators, I figured it was a bomb but I didn't know what sort of bomb, this must be what it was all for. They're using my plans to try and do this cure you talk about! Oh Fuck and I brought it all right to them... on a silver fucking platter how fucking stupid was I to think they weren't going to kill Kurt and me anyway.

LUTHER
Oh my fucking God! Look, she's deluded okay, I give you that but this girl I talked about, she can help us, she can help us stop this.

WESTON
WHAT? Man, you said she was in on it.

LUTHER
Yes, she was, but she was, it's hard to explain but, she was like deceived and led astray, she's ignorant she just doesn't know the magnitude of what she's involved in.

WESTON
What? How can you be sure?

LUTHER
I was chained an dying in that chamber like you were and she got me out when it was against the wishes of the people doing it.

WESTON
HOW!? How do we stop anything? We can just go now, run.

LUTHER
How far do you think we're going to get, no food, no water, no transport.
(MORE)

89 CONTINUED: (6) 89

LUTHER (CONT'D)
And aren't you listening to me, I'm one of them I mean physically, I need weekly doses of heat and if I am exposed to temperatures under 26 degrees I basically die. They're tearing the town apart as we speak, killing innocent people... If you wanna go Weston... I won't blame you... but I can't, so it's either I die from the bomb or from leaving...so I have to stop this bomb.

LUTHER gets up, and starts to walk away.

WESTON
I guess I have nothing left to lose, and I don't want to become infected with this condition or whatever it is you talk about, assuming I'm not infected already.

WESTON and **LUTHER** pick up a jog as they run back towards the town.

90 INT. HARRY'S GARAGE KIOSK BUILDING. VERY EARLY MORNING. 90

We are back in **HARRY'S** living room. We see all the carnage, **NANCY** lies there under the sofa in a weak, beaten heap. She moans softly in pain. The camera stops when it gets close to **NANCY.**

-- In **HARRY'S** bedroom -- A shot is seen of **HARRY** sitting in his bed-room. He stares at the floor. He gets up and then sits back down again. He exhales deeply, he looks out the window to the side thinking.

BACK TO:

91 EXT. OUTSIDE HARRY'S GARAGE. VERY EARLY MORNING. 91

LUTHER and **WESTON** run up behind the back of **HARRY'S** kiosk building. They both walk bent over at the waist to avoid windows. They slink along until they reach another window.

WESTON
(In a whisper.)
What room is this?

(CONTINUED)

LUTHER
It’s Nancy’s bedroom

LUTHER slowly stands up to the right of the window, he slowly peers in, he sees no one. He gestures to **WESTON** and they keep moving. They move to the next window and **LUTHER** does likewise.

What he sees: The trashed room with blood in certain places. **LUTHER** covers his mouth and closes his eyes.

LUTHER
OH MY GOD!!!

WESTON
What!? What is it?!

LUTHER
(Crying.)
I think he’s killed Nancy.

WESTON
Oh, I’m sorry man... really.

They are both interrupted with a whine inside. **LUTHER** looks back in.

What he sees: **NANCY** has managed to worm her way out from under the sofa and wiggle over to the window. She looks up at the window, still bloodied and gagged. The guys speak in loud, determined and raspy whispers here.

LUTHER
Weston you have to go round and knock on his door or something to distract him.

WESTON
What!? I-

LUTHER
Just run back here once you’ve done it I need to keep an eye on Nancy, please!

WESTON
Shut up listen!

LUTHER and **WESTON** look round as they hear a vehicle approaching.

91 CONTINUED: (2) 91

LUTHER stands at the window and signs to her to hush. **LUTHER** leaps back down again. **HARRY** walks into the room. He walks over to **NANCY**, he looks at the window and locks it. He walks over to **NANCY** when a knock at the door distracts him.

The knocking is relentless and very loud. **HARRY** leaves the room again to go and answer the door.

HARRY goes to answer the door.

-- At **HARRY'S** front door -- **HARRY** answers it. **IVY MIKE** stands there, with his truck in the back ground, idling.

IVY MIKE
(Humbled.)
Harry, we couldn't find no one...
and Grable's bin'hurt real bad.

HARRY looks over **IVY MIKE'S** shoulder in what we can now start to recognize as fury.

IVY MIKE
They have to have run into the
desert Harry, and if they have it
doesn't matter, they'll be dead
within a day or two.

HARRY
You dumb fucking dunce.

92 INT. NANCY'S BEDROOM. NIGHT. 92

From inside: a brick flies through the window.

-- AT THE FRONT DOOR -- **HARRY** looks round hearing this.

-- IN NANCY'S ROOM -- **LUTHER** scrambles in through the window, getting a few cuts on the way in. **NANCY** wails, muffled through her gag. **LUTHER** picks her up and takes her through the window.

WESTON
(Through window.)
COME ON!!!

WESTON helps **LUTHER** lift **NANCY** outside.

92 CONTINUED: 92

HARRY goes back to **NANCY'S** bedroom, **IVY MIKE** follows and sees the broken window and that **NANCY** is gone.

HARRY
You're truck...

IVY MIKE
What?

HARRY
You're truck still has the keys in it.

93 EXT. OUTSIDE HARRY'S HOUSE. NIGHT. 93

LUTHER, WESTON and **NANCY** bundle into Ivy Mike's truck. They see the engine is idling. They reverse.

94 INT. HARRY'S HOUSE. NIGHT. 94

At the front door **HARRY** and **IVY MIKE** can see that **NANCY** and co. have of course made away in **MIKES'** truck.

IVY MIKE
Harry, I'll fix this I-

HARRY lurches forward grabbing **IVY MIKE'S** head and crushes **IVY MIKE'S** face with his hands with crushing strength.

95 EXT. NEVADA DESERT. VERY EARLY MORNING. 95

WESTON, LUTHER and **NANCY** speed along the track in Ivy Mike's pick-up truck. They arrive in town. It is very silent.

WESTON
Why is it so silent.

NANCY
They do this for some reason when Uncle Harry has business in the town. Take the fourth left up here. Here, turn in here.

The truck turns in down another side street, they drive to a storage shed.

95 CONTINUED: 95

NANCY
Get out!

They do.

96 INT. HARRY'S HOUSE. VERY EARLY MORNING. 96

HARRY talks on his walkie talkie.

97 EXT. ELSEWHERE IN TOWN. VERY EARLY MORNING. 97

One of the muscle men we saw in the diner at the beginning, watching **LUTHER**, **PALUMBO**, stands with his back to a building on his walkie-talkie.

PALUMBO
Yeah, Harry?

98 INT. HARRY'S HOUSE. VERY EARLY MORNING. 98

HARRY
Palumbo, they're in Mike's truck.

PALUMBO
On it.

HARRY
Good.

99 EXT. OUTSIDE STORAGE SHED. EARLY MORNING. 99

NANCY goes over to the door on the storage shed. It's barred shut. **NANCY** walks over to a pile of tires next to the right hand-side door and reaches into the pile. She brings out a key.

WESTON
(In a sharp whisper.)
How the hell did you know the key was there.

NANCY
When I was a little girl, I used to help Harry and the guys unload things and clean-up, we always kept the key here.

99 CONTINUED: 99

WESTON
What are we here for? We can't hide in here.

NANCY
We ain't here to hide, we're here to get protection!

NANCY unlocks the door. She reaches round and gropes for the light switch.

The coils in the light-bulb erupt into a sickly orange glow. The character's faces, bodies and the entire house is a bright and unnatural orange. Shots are seen of different areas in the shed.

NANCY
Now, Harry said that they store the liquid nitrogen coolants in here.

WESTON
Do you know where the bomb is?

NANCY
No, Harry never let me near it.

The two men look in hopelessness.

LUTHER
We'll find it!

WESTON
What do they look like? The canisters? What type.

NANCY
I-I dunno, just big silver canisters I think.

WESTON
Why do you have liquid nitrogen in a shed?

NANCY
It's industrial coolant for machinery of all sorts.

WESTON
Look, why are we doing this, why don't we-

99 CONTINUED: (2) 99

NANCY
-Look I dunno, everything okay! I just know that this will kill my family!

The two men realize the enormity of the ask as that is basically what these men are to her.

NANCY rummages around.

NANCY
Ah! Yes here they are.

Three enormous canisters are seen.

WESTON
(To Nancy.)
Are there any smaller canisters?

NANCY
YES! YES! When Dr. Oppenheimer left Harry took the pharmaceutical canisters.

WESTON
Are they in here?

NANCY
Uh, yes... they should be over here.

She rummages some more towards the back of the shed.

NANCY
Got them uh...

WESTON
-Weston.

NANCY
Weston. Harry keeps his piping over there.

LUTHER
How is this gonna work?

NANCY
Easy, just attach the nozzle of the pressurised liquid nitrogen into a tap washer, here I got some of those too-

99 CONTINUED: (3) 99

NANCY pours some out of her apron pockets.

LUTHER walks back over to the door to check no one is watching.

They all hold their clothes over their mouths. They go about making the connections **NANCY** mentions. The cannisters go through the washers from the tanks into piping similar to hose pipes.

NANCY
The cold will perish the material in a few hours so we have to be real careful when we use it.

WESTON
We should set a distraction. This shed is full of gas-

WESTON points to BBQ gas canisters on a large shelf.

WESTON
-I say we torch it and flush them all out. You go outside and I'll set it up.

NANCY
Yes! And here...

NANCY gives her cigarette lighter to **WESTON.**

NANCY and **LUTHER** exit the shed. **WESTON** opens all their nozzles, covering his mouth with his sleeve. **WESTON** shouts to them from inside.

WESTON
I've opened them all up now.

WESTON goes to the entrance and ignites **NANCY'S** lighter, then throws it in and runs away.

100 EXT. OUTSIDE STORAGE SHED. NIGHT. 100

The three of them duck. A huge explosion followed by a plume of fire billows out of the store shed, they dive out of the way. The structure quickly disintegrates into a collapsed bonfire.

(CONTINUED)

100 CONTINUED: 100

NANCY
When they come, we need to drive them into a house, there we can blocke'm off at both ends and freeze 'em there.

CUT TO:

101 EXT. OUT-SIDE BURNING SHED. VERY EARLY MORNING. 101

A group of **HARRY'S** men stand outside inspecting the fire.

102 INT. HEAT CHAMBER. NIGHT. 102

HARRY and a few more of his men crouch on the ground. **HARRY** opens a trap door that was previously invisible. He pulls out some strange looking devices that look like DIY flamethrowers. **HARRY** activates one and shoots a jet of flame from it to test it, we can see that flamethrowers is exactly what they are.

103 EXT. BACK YARD OF HOUSE. NIGHT. 103

LUTHER and co. tip-toe through the back yard of a house until they reach a back door. **WESTON** gives a signal and **LUTHER** and **NANCY** storm in.

104 INT. HOUSE. NIGHT. 104

LUTHER wields his weapon and shouts for the residents to get out, no one stirs. **LUTHER** emerges out of a room.

LUTHER
(To Nancy.)
Where are they?

NANCY
They seem to have a system of knowing when a test is going to happen and they hide in their safe rooms when this happens, I hear most folks in most of the valleys do this.

WESTON
Is a test going to happen?

104 CONTINUED: 104

NANCY
Yeah, I think so, a few valleys over.

LUTHER
I've got an idea.

105 EXT. STREET. NIGHT. 105

HARRY and his men, have now been joined by **CASTLE BRAVO** and **GRABLE,** who's face is grossly swollen, black and blue and crudely bandaged. They are warmly dressed and proceed through the street all wielding these flame throwers, they stop when a sparking toaster hangs out of a window by its cable.

106 INT. HOUSE. NIGHT. 106

The house is quite dark apart from a few lamps. **LUTHER** and co. walk into the living room and kitchen areas.

107 EXT. HOUSE. NIGHT. 107

LUTHER runs out of the back door and round the side and stands in the frame of the front door. **LUTHER** sees **HARRY** and his crew inspecting the sparking toaster at the front. He scooshes his freezing cold spray at them, Harry's men scream in shock and one of the muscle men is hit on the leg and screams in pain. **WESTON** follows this up by shattering the frozen leg of one of Harry's men by striking it with a tire iron. He Steals the flame thrower from him.

HARRY and his men let fly with the flamethrowers, igniting non-heat resistant **WESTON'S** sleeve forcing **WESTON** to run out of the house trying to put the fire of his sleeve out.

LUTHER fires his stream of cold and **HARRY** his stream of fire, the two streams meet, creating enormous clouds of thick steam. All of them take advantage of this. **HARRY** and his men run for the back door and **LUTHER** for the front.

HARRY and the remaining men let loose with their flame throwers.

107 CONTINUED: 107

LUTHER and his friends run away down an alley, but Luther stops, he turns round. He realises the only way he can stop the bomb being detonated is to stop Harry.

WESTON
What are you doing.

LUTHER
There's only one way we're going to stop this bomb.

HARRY realizes this is over and beckons to his remaining men.

108 INT. HEAT CHAMBER. NIGHT. 108

HARRY and his remaining men give themselves a heat dose in the heat chamber. But this time, a civilian is strapped up in a cross shape attached to the floor and roof, the furnace blasts fire at the civilian incinerating him and ash and particles from the body blast through the mesh onto **HARRY** and his men.

BACK TO:

109 EXT. TOWNSHIP. DAWN. 109

HARRY stands with his snake rattle in the middle of the street looking at our group of heros. Camera holds on both for a few beats each.

LUTHER'S face is seen. It runs with sweat, blood and tears.

Close on: **HARRY'S** face is seen. Stony and emotionless.

NANCY and **WESTON** reflect just as much desperation as **LUTHER.**

110 EXT. TOWN. DAWN. 110

HARRY takes out his rattle snake rattle, and throws it to the ground. Symbolically he is now the rattle incarnate.

LUTHER turns round to **NANCY** and **WESTON.**

LUTHER
You two stay right here... they won't hurt you anymore.

WESTON
W-what-

LUTHER
Stay here.

NANCY
No Luther!-

LUTHER
Please just stay here. If you die, this will have been all for nothing.

LUTHER walks out into the street with his tank. **HARRY'S** men wait in respect for the symbolical deciding moment between one camp and the other.

LUTHER passes the stolen flame thrower to **NANCY** and takes his shirt off.

LUTHER
Fire it at me.

NANCY does so. She scooshes the fire around his torso, **LUTHER** walks round on the spot taking the fire. **NANCY** finishes. **HARRY** and his men exchange glances realizing that trying to kill **LUTHER** with fire was futile.

HARRY bellows and spreads his arms.

A brutal fight to the death ensues. **HARRY** throws **LUTHER** around like a cloth, sometimes with one arm. After a while. **HARRY** takes out his knife. **WESTON** sees this and throws **LUTHER'S** freezing weapon towards him. **LUTHER** sprays **HARRY** in the face with the cold. **LUTHER** hits **HARRY** over the head with the canister, shattering his head, **HARRY** falls to the ground. **LUTHER** kneels over **HARRY** and continues to shatter **HARRY'S** head with the canister until he is sure that **HARRY** is dead.

LUTHER looks up and sees **HARRY'S** men are running off into the desert.

LUTHER gets up, very sore and limps back to his friends. When he gets to them.

110 CONTINUED: (2) 110

WESTON
What? They're going?

LUTHER
No... their going to detonate the bomb.

NANCY
We can stop them!

LUTHER hobbles back over to **HARRY'S** corpse. He grabs **HARRY'S** arm.

WESTON
What are you doing?

LUTHER takes Harry's meat knife from one of his pockets, and hacks into Harry's wrist, cutting it off. He picks up Harry's flamethrowers and scooshes the hand with a jet of fire. The hand remains unharmed. **LUTHER** smiles.

LUTHER
GOOD... WESTON! Take this hand and show it to your scientist friends and bring back help and a solution if you possibly can because we're not gonna last long without-

WESTON
-I know, - I know.

WESTON nods. He takes the hand. Next **WESTON** looks over to and starts in the direction of where Ivy Mike's truck was parked. **LUTHER** stops **WESTON** for a moment.

LUTHER
(To Nancy.)
Go, go with him!

NANCY
No Luther! You can come too!

LUTHER
NO! GO! GO WITH HIM! NOW! GO! As I said, if anything happens to either of you it will all be wasted, I think I can still stop this, but I want you to go I'm not risking your life any more.

LUTHER pushes her away towards **WESTON**.

110 CONTINUED: (3) 110

LUTHER
Please! You'll be safe with our friend! Go Now! GO! GO!

NANCY, very upset runs with **WESTON** to go and get the truck. **LUTHER** still bellowing for them to go can still be heard off screen.

LUTHER starts to run in the direction that Harry's men were running in. On his way he screams out to all the town to whoever might be listening or within ear shot.

LUTHER
AN ATOMIC BOMB IS GOING TO GO OFF!!! EVERYBODY GET OUT OF YOUR HOUSES!!! AND RUN!!!!!

Nothing happens in the town, so **LUTHER** gives up shouting and keeps running himself.

LUTHER
GEEETTT OUUTT!!!!!!!!!!

111 EXT. BOMB TOWER. DAWN. 111

GRABLE pulls on a chain connected to a huge suspended component near the war head. The device clangs on the metal around it.

BACK TO:

112 EXT. NEVADA DESERT. EARLY MORNING. 112

LUTHER charging through the desert. He can still hear the massive clank reverberating.

BACK TO:

113 EXT. BOMB TOWER. DAWN. 113

GRABLE slowly guides a metal cylinder into the side of the bomb.

BACK TO:

114 EXT. HARRY'S GARAGE. DAWN. 114

WESTON and **NANCY** arrive at Harry's garage. **NANCY** jumps off and runs to the heat chamber. **WESTON,** in a spray of dust from the rear tire speeds off past the garage and into the desert.

BACK TO:

115 EXT. DESERT. DAWN. 115

LUTHER runs and pants and lurches forward running through his pain. The scene goes to silence for a few beats with only **LUTHER'S** sounds heard. A few moments later a huge white flash envelopes the screen.

The screen remains white for a few beats. Next the white fades away, it reveals a shot of **LUTHER** running away from the enormous mushroom cloud behind him. Most of the sky is taken up with the mushroom cloud.

LUTHER runs even harder, the clothes on his back start to ignite with the heat. The shock wave of bomb gaining on **LUTHER** and the bang of the bombs sound waves reverberating millions of times per second between the O-Zone layer and the ground screams out.

116 EXT. TEST WATCHMANS OFFICE. DAWN. 116

At the site of the other test. A **TEST WATCHMAN** looks with binoculars over at the other glow in the sky in the other valley, Luther and co's valley.

117 EXT. DESERT. DAWN. 117

Panorama of the explosion is seen. The mushroom tumbles into the sky. The shock wave can be seen travelling in a perfect circle away from the bomb. The shock wave flattens and decimates all in its path.

The rest of Harry's men we saw run out into the desert are in their five mile from ground zero sweet spot. They stand in a row in their heat chamber pose the shock wave reaches them and vaporizes them.

The town is flattened and taken out.

(CONTINUED)

117 CONTINUED: 117

Harry's garage has it's roof blown off.

118 INT. HEAT CHAMBER. DAWN. 118

NANCY screams in fright inside.

BACK TO:

119 EXT. DESERT. DAWN. 119

WESTON'S truck is buffeted and is lifted off the ground for a bit.

120 INT. WESTON'S TRUCK. DAWN 120

WESTON looks round aghast at the mushroom cloud out his back window.

121 EXT. DESERT. DAWN. 121

WESTON then powers into the distance.

FADE TO:

122 EXT. OUTSIDE HEAT CHAMBER. DAWN. 122

NANCY stands out-side of the heat chamber whilst a very powerful nuclear wind blows her hair. A blood and dust caked **LUTHER** hobbles up to her. They embrace and segue into a passionate kiss. They part.

NANCY
He was still my Uncle Harry.

LUTHER nods, understanding the strange and inevitable attachment that happens in these cases where an innocent lives with a psychopath.

DISSOLVE TO:

123 EXT. OUTSIDE HEAT CHAMBER. DAWN. 123

A shot is seen of a little thermometer on the heat chamber. It reads only ten degrees.

(CONTINUED)

123 CONTINUED: 123

LUTHER comes out of the heat chamber wrapped in blankets and looks out into the desert. He sees a little thermometer attached to the outside of the chamber. He picks it up and looks at it, perplexed, it reads only ten degrees Celsius. He holds it to his ear and shakes it then considers for a beat.

Camera cuts to farther and farther away shots of the heat chamber. The final shot taking in the remnants of the mushroom cloud in the distance.

ROLL CREDITS.

THE END.

22027269R00068

Printed in Great Britain
by Amazon